Personality Disorders in the Criminal Justice System

ALICIA WILCOX

ISBN: 1-7990-5294-X
ISBN-13: 9781799052944

CONTENTS

ACKNOWLEDGMENTS

I would like to acknowledge all of the forensic psychologists, researchers, professors and everyone that has worked with me throughout this book, as well as the entirety of those who, in the face of adversity, have refused to turn a blind eye toward the personality disorder epidemic.

INTRODUCTION

For centuries, individuals with Antisocial Personality Disorder have captivated society. From murder documentaries to mystery novels, the "psychopath" has become a pop culture phenomenon. Although this highly publicized figure is currently identified through the examination of scary films or crime shows, this is not how they can be spotted in real life. ASPD has been largely misunderstood ever since history has been able to document. Many are intrigued by this disorder, since mystery has always been a large component. The questions that remain about these individuals cannot be taken care of by one single answer, and the actuality is more complex than most can comprehend. In fact, those all the way from forensic psychologists to mental health professionals have remained dumb-founded when attempting to treat, diagnose, or simply handle the disorder. This universality of the confusion does not call for dismissal, and shall not be set aside, but instead looked into on a deeper level. In the assessment of one's personality disorder, one must put any prior judgments aside and strive to understand the mindset of the effected individual in the clearest way possible, no matter how unsettling.

As early as 1801, those considered "insane" began to appear in the research and literature of many theorists. Pinel coined the term "manie sans délire" to describe one that shows antisocial behaviors without actually appearing to be insane. Before this, individuals considered to be insane had to show evidence of hallucinations or delusions. The main factor that captivates the psychological community regarding "sociopaths" and "psychopaths" is the absence of any intellectual impairment. While many would like to believe that those with personality disorders are malfunctioning intellectually, many are completely normal. This is why their behavior and emotional mindsets must not be ignored, but looked into even more carefully.

Moving forward, in 1897, Maudsley proposed that when it comes to those with ASPD, it was "useless to punish those that cannot control their behavior." This would shortly be followed by a less than sympathetic approach: the implementation of mental asylums. Yet, later on, his proposal of questioning the use of punishment would later spark the current movement of speculation in regards to punishment's impact. That being said, for a long while, asylums were look at as a last resort due to the fact that these individuals were viewed as hopelessly incurable. Yet, the asylums were imposed as a first resort. Not only was this costly, but it did nothing to improve the behavior of those thought of as insane, since they were deemed incurable from the start. Later on, in 1968, the DSM-2 began the term Antisocial Personality Disorder, and dropped the idea of the "dyssocial sociopath" leaving one with nothing but the antisocial one. Those with Antisocial Personality Disorder showed the personality traits of one who was thought to be a sociopath or psychopath, the terms often being used interchangeably. It is imperative, from the beginning, to note the difference: sociopaths are raised, and psychopaths are born. Both have Antisocial Personality Disorder. On a more general level, since those with ASPD are not intellectually disabled, the symptoms of the disorder can only be seen in a derangement involving the emotions, feelings and morals. Although their conscience is virtually absent, most are high functioning and are able to continue to carry themselves successfully in society. A lot of the time, the general absence in their moral compass does not result in violent behavior, but rather the lack of empathy and emotional responses as a whole. These individuals go through the motions of their lives, often bored, indifferent, and sometimes manipulative, contradicting the belief that they are always violent and dangerous. It must be recognized that the symptoms of ASPD, contrary to popular belief, are often invisible.

Quite recently, the terms "sociopath" and "psychopath" have been deemed incorrect, and only Antisocial Personality Disorder has remained, although the terms sociopath and psychopath continue to be mildly used in various settings. That being said, those attempting to be politically correct by labeling these terms as "offensive" must consider: although it is crucial to show psychological respect, these individuals are not the type to take offense, and the ones who will be offended by "incorrect" terminology can be taken off the list of having this disorder. Furthermore, the eradication of offensive terminology regarding disorders is nothing but a mere pattern of history. It is not the term itself that is offensive, but the negative connotation that is placed onto the term, that then causes society to be offended. That being said, in the history of Antisocial Personality Disorder, the terminology is the least alarming component. However, until society strives to eradicate the stigma around Antisocial Personality Disorder, people worldwide will continue to be taken aback by *anything* said about "psychopaths".

In the past decade, ASPD has increased from 3% to 6.2%. To put this in perspective, one can observe how many vegans they know, because more people have Antisocial Personality Disorder. This disorder is as big a problem as alcoholism, yet rarely pondered over. Not only that, but solutions are almost never talked about as an option, let alone considered. The general public, and even informed experts, label the effected individuals as incurable. What society needs is an incentive to change that. Refusing to inquire further or continue the research regarding such an extensive problem is not only foolish, but entails many future consequences. Since these types of personalities are growing within the general population, it is one's responsibility, whether that be as a theorist, researcher, therapist, or intellectual searching for answers, to acknowledge the truth of their presence, as well as attempt to either decrease their extensiveness or improve their current state.

Social condemnation is often a quick and seamless way to handle those considered to be insane. And yet, ever since the early 1800's, controversial observations have been made about those with ASPD. Many have been stunned when studying those who have qualified to be considered maniacs. When faced with the fact that their level of understanding is not impaired, many are speechless, wondering how they can continue their destructive behavior knowing the effect that it has.

CHAPTER ONE – ANTISOCIAL PERSONALITY DISORDER

There does exist a type of mental abnormality in which the main problem lies in the malfunctioning of one's emotions. While the individual experiences no impairment involving reasoning abilities or intellectual capacity, the moral compass is almost non-existent, except what the individual has picked up and learned from their peers through careful and meticulous observation. Because of this complete lack of sentiments towards others, this individual is able to smoothly pave their way through almost any situation, without regards for what may occur afterwards. He quickly learns, through the examination of others, what is expected of him, and follows that guide of what he comes to believe is correct. This constant act becomes his way of life, and he is suddenly able to conduct himself with righteousness throughout his social interactions. And what is more, he is able to get his way through his use of manipulative charm and social tactics. Nothing may fully satisfy him, since he cannot experience joy on the same depth that a neurotypical may. Because of this, he quickly moves from one objective to the next, with no regard for the other individual involved in the social interaction. He experiences a proneness to boredom, and feels indifferent toward everything. This motivates him to engage in any type of activity that has the chance of stimulating the mind. Manipulation often temporarily cures this said boredom, ending in the other individual being discarded once he finds a new objective to become involved with. This is their cycle, and these individuals often engage in seemingly lowkey social interactions that end with large-scale consequences, yet keep it on the down low, effortlessly.

It is out of the question for him to have even a minimal fascination with disaster or delight. He is indifferent to the matters that make up humanity, as can be seen in real life or fictional stories. These stories have the power to move others, but not him. The stories are not incapable—he is. Likewise, he is often unable to see, or indifferent to the fact that other people have emotional reactions. Although no impairment to his intelligence exists, he is handicapped—blind, in the sense that he cannot be conscious to the emotions of the human species. Even a wordy explanation of how one's feelings operate will not resonate with him, since he possesses no personal experience to base it off of. He cannot learn, and potentially never will, since he does not hope to understand.

The characteristics that constitute ASPD can often be seen in day-to-day social interactions, simple conversations—not heinous crimes. In 1915, Kraepelin defined the psychopath as "a criminal by impulse who is overcome by an uncontrollable desire to commit crimes". Others came into the debate to argue that they were professional criminals—acting out of self-interest rather than uncontrollable impulses. Quite frequently, these personalities lack remorse in socially acceptable ways. Their main qualities: lack of morals, no remorse, absence of a conscience, are manifested in ways that are socially embraced, and almost invisible, towards the others interacting with them, even family. They navigate their way through life manifesting their disadvantages into advantages, being able to go through the motions without any emotional aspects involved. Although they do not experience delusions or possess any criteria that qualifies them to be considered insane, they do possess a level of what is claimed by many to be moral insanity. This moral insanity is what allows them to engage in such antisocial behaviors. What causes this moral insanity, however, has sparked widespread confusion for generations.

Many psychologists hypothesize that some are more naturally prone to Antisocial Personality Disorder than others due to their environment. This is why rehabilitations in prisons is not often attempted, since their behavior is hypothesized to be adaptive—a result of their need to adapt to a harmful environment from a young age. Going off of this belief, that moral imbecility is their destiny, punishment shows no effect on the "psychopath". Although some believe that the cause of a lack in morals is hereditary, this would also support the belief that heredity is a crucial factor in the development of a conscience, thus supporting the idea that a childhood environment fosters the growth of the "psychopathic" child. Keeping this in mind, many have examined that one's morals and ethics are learned, and that learning process is enforced by their emotions toward the values that are being enforced within them. If, in adulthood, these emotions are lacking, we can conclude that the development has been jeopardized—the learning process has been tampered with—which leads many to believe that one's environment, is in fact, responsible. Because of this lack of emotion, there is nothing to guide the actions of the "psychopath" besides the eternal boredom that he experiences. Because he is a "psychopath" he will do things that are seen as terrible towards the general public. However, it is crucial to note that although "psychopaths" do terrible things, just because someone does terrible things, does not mean that they are a "psychopath" themselves.

The types of environments that require a child to adapt in such ways that involve the eradication of emotions should be inquired further into and examined in order to stop the disorder from rising. The knowledge about the environment that may cause ASPD can prevent the disorder from occurring in one's life. Not only will this save the life of the individual at hand, but will save the life of anyone that associates with the individual in the future.

Antisocial Personality Disorder today, in the current DSM, is defined as: individuals who habitually and pervasively disregard or violate the rights and considerations of others without remorse. The current diagnostic criteria involves diagnosing an individual with many of the following characteristics: glibness, superficial charm, grandiose sense of self worth, failure to accept responsibility of one's actions, proneness to boredom, etc. With this in mind, it is important for those diagnosing, as well as anybody, to keep in mind that the finding of one or more of these traits does not call for a diagnosis. In fact, a low level of these traits can be found in the average person. That being said, even in the event of a possible diagnosis, other factors not including, and on top of these personality traits must also be taken into consideration. Antisocial Personality Disorder is not one dimensional, and is more complex than the discovery of an individual who seems arrogant from an outside perspective glance. The term antisocial, in a psychological aspect, refers to the psychological/behavioral component of the personality disorder. Antisocial behavior means that one is acting disruptively and doing things that go against the norm. It indicates that one is violating the social norm, contrary to the belief that it refers to one being shy or introverted. The term antisocial, in this case, will always refer to the individual's behavior that is seen as unacceptable. Those who have ASPD know the difference between right and wrong, they just don't care. In regards to their "antisocial" behavior, they are constantly aware of the fact that their actions are illogical and out of the norm. Their reasoning and intellectual skills are perfectly intact, they just don't care about the potential consequences. This makes the "psychopath" that much more intriguing, since they continue to engage in such antisocial behavior without feeling any remorse or guilt after the fact. This being the case, one can conclude that the individual's ability to eliminate all emotion aspects in any given situation is the factor that allows them to do almost everything that they desire, since they will not be plagued with any possible guilt or regret afterwards.

It is incorrect to assert that unusual behavior permits a diagnosis of ASPD, since the symptoms seem to be less than observable. On the outside, these individuals function quite well within society. On the inside, morals are not present, and a conscience does not, in fact, guide their behavior. Looking further on an interpersonal level, the "psychopath" is unable to form deep bonds with others. He lacks guilt, remorse, and is often superficial and manipulative. This makes these individuals more prone to antisocial behaviors, yet the majority of these characteristics mentioned are not easy to spot. They are intentionally kept well hidden within the psyche of the individual, while simultaneously being the main guide for their actions. To the surprise of some, many who have ASPD never become involved with the criminal justice system, and there is a noteworthy gap between these individuals and their criminal peers. Although they live with the same disorder, different levels of this disorder can be found within each individual, and it is never black and white. This complexity—this grayness—can be seen in the trouble that occurs when attempting to diagnose one with the disorder. The diagnostic criteria for the disorder remains broad, and it is easy for one to claim that an individual might have Antisocial Personality Disorder. Although this makes it easier on therapists and criminal psychologists, there is much at stake for the individual at hand. Later on, the consequences and processes that occur after a diagnosis of ASPD will be discussed. For now, it is imperative to keep in mind that internal mental processes are just as, if not more important to research as external behaviors.

Universal confusion surrounds the behaviors that constitute Antisocial Personality Disorder. Is a psychopath a morbid liar? Is a sociopath violent? Although various levels of ASPD can be seen, many of those with the disorder are quite glib and charming. This ties into their manipulative skill set. If they consistently lashed out and acted different from the typical person, it would be clear that they were different themselves. Often times, it is not clear at all. Ultimately, one should not be so quick to diagnose Antisocial Personality Disorder when, for centuries, the diagnostic criteria has remained so unclear. Since this diagnostic criteria has been vague throughout history, it is also unclear as to whether or not treatment is possible. Nonetheless, people everywhere are quick to jump to the conclusion that "psychopaths" are hopeless individuals, even though so little about their disorder is known. Just the diagnosis of Antisocial Personality Disorder itself carries with it the notion of hopelessness. In fact, those that try for treatment are looked at as foolish, and treatment itself is often seen as a waste of time. However, it is understandable that the individual's family and friends would seek to find a cure. Further research would be the first step, in order to shed light on many of the misunderstood aspects of this disorder. This would also ease the worries of those who are wary about knowing someone affected by ASPD.

Almost any theory that has been put up regarding Antisocial Personality Disorder has been widely debated. The aftermath of their behavior, however, remains clear. This individual continues to follow the path that their indifference and apathetic attitude takes them on. In order to experience any slight stimulation, they will enter almost any situation without regards to the end result. This is the irony of their lifestyle, since no activity ever ends in an emotional response. With that set aside, this individual often appears to be more than intelligent towards his peers—being able to give each person the exact, calculated response that they will most desperately desire. His false affections will be thrown onto others, and yet later on the individuals that interacted with this person will be left much worse than before. The aftermath will not be visible, since the "psychopath" will effortlessly justify any behavior, no matter how antisocial it may be. He will go to great lengths to move the attention towards his targets, and away from any trouble he may have caused, thus shutting out the idea that he has done anything wrong in the first place.

CHAPTER TWO – THE DIAGONISTIC CRITERIA FOR ASPD

The diagnostic criteria of the "psychopath" is evolving and up for debate. There have been drastic transitions in the development of the psychopath. Diving into a deeper intellectual understanding of Antisocial Personality Disorder is crucial to building an accurate understanding of the current definition. Not only is it important to define the disorder, but it is necessary to come to conclusions on how one should handle ASPD, as well as any personality disorder, as an individual and as a society. Yet, society today is far from doing so. Criminal psychologists and mental health professionals remain dumb-founded—not only when diagnosing, but when attempting to treat their clients with ASPD. It is imperative that all people delve deeper into what it means to be a "psychopath" so that juries can be properly educated, those with the disorder can be treated in a humane manner, the list goes on.

Coming to a conclusion about how to deal with these individuals can only be done once the definition comes to a full standing. For now, the characteristics that constitute ASPD remain broad, and the definition remains vague. Once the psychological aspects are fully understood, treatment opportunities will be made more clear. Currently, any attempt of treatment is thought of as unrealistic, and most efforts end up swept under the rug. The stigma around Antisocial Personality Disorder must be altered—misunderstandings surrounding "psychopathy" should be eradicated as well.

For all of history, psychologists have been perplexed by the mental state of "insanity" that exclusively involves a deterioration of morals. Individuals that fell under the category of this disorder were primarily viewed as savages in society. Now, on a more accurate plane, one might recognize them as the successful CEOs. The mental image that comes to mind when the word "psychopath" is uttered has changed drastically over the course of time. While one has previously labeled them as vicious and violent, it has been figured out that they may be more narcissistic and detached. Although one with ASPD may be violent, a separate individual with the same, identical disorder may have no violent tendencies at all. This discovery added to the clinical idea of what warranted a diagnosis of insanity. "Psychopaths" did not fit the criteria to be insane, since they had no psychosis, and their mental illness derived solely from a malfunctioning in morals and emotions. Although they engage in abnormal behaviors, they are not always wicked or vicious beings. While the psychopathic man used to be defined as uncontrollable and impulsive, he is thought of, now, to be nothing but apathetic— wandering through life without the weight of emotional baggage.

The eternal confusion that has surrounded psychopathy for centuries must be demystified. What is being done to handle these individuals must be not only conversed, but also looked into in order to reach a final and consistent conclusion. Not only does the treatment of these individuals affect the mental health system, but the criminal justice one as well.

Based on the current understanding, it is not crazy to say that the majority of "psychopaths" never end up in the criminal justice system. Rather, they can be seen in typical settings, most of them never engaging in criminal activity throughout their lives. The higher functioning, the more likely they are to notice, quite quickly, that the antisocial behavior their thoughts tempt them with will end in consequences detrimental to their reputation. Individuals who are lower functioning know the consequences as well, yet disregard them and continue to engage in destructive behavior, curing their boredom with any hopes to see the downfall of others. With that in mind, further research is imperative, since a diagnosis of ASPD permanently alters the life of the individual affected as well as others involved.

From the original emergence to its current exhibition, Antisocial Personality Disorder has left many in a state of astonishment. People wonder who around them is at stake. Those who know the answer to this, then face the question of how to deal with it. For now, these individuals are treated as threats to one's own safety, which does nothing but shoots down any opportunity to help them use their disorder for the greater good.

CHAPTER THREE – HOW ASPD CAN BE USED TO ONE'S ADVANTAGE

The confusion that surrounds the decision-making process of what to do about psychopaths is null compared to the confusion that surrounds those who view their behavior as beneficial. Many theorize that if their behavior is a result of a previous toxic environment, that behavior is an adaptation. Since the behavior is adaptive, some assume that it has helpful qualities. There are many patterns in the human anatomy that are proof of useless adaptations. For instance, certain organs, like the appendix, have been contained throughout generations, yet show no clear use. Although their behavior may be adaptive, that does not imply that it is beneficial to the human species. In fact, the human species as a whole would be better off without these individuals. Their actions are pathologies—they show *inflexibility* towards adaptations. What's adaptive for one party may promote the destruction of another. Their behavior is, some of the time, a result of their environment. This is a huge indicator of hope, because it proves that it is preventable. A disorder first thought of as so foreign and unexplainable, now, is seen undergoing a transformation of increasing understanding from outside perspectives.

Since antisocial characteristics have not yet been effectively terminated from a large size of the population, an easy coping mechanism for those who surround the psychopath is to affirm that society needs them. They claim that communities are dependent on their unique behavior. At the end of the day, though, it is quantitatively obvious that the antisocial individual does more harm than good. Although they may be able to solve problems more seamlessly than the average individual, they end up producing more problems in the first place than ever solving them. After all, someone without morals cannot function more effectively than those who *do* possess a conscience. Although no antisocial characteristics have been eradicated in a large size of the population, various treatments have proven effective in different individuals. These "cured" individuals act as a testament towards the effectiveness, as well as hopefulness, regarding treatment. These people show that the characteristics of ASPD are better of non-existent, and one must strive to terminate them instead of keep them alive out of hopelessness.

That being said, if a multitude of solutions are found to be unhelpful in curing the psychopath, one can be then left with the option to teach the individual how to utilize their unique behaviors in society in order to benefit their community. From the workplace or a family environment, many antisocial traits allow the individual to do things that others would not be able to. They are able to sacrifice one person in order to save a larger group. They are able to do things that are immoral—things that others would be too uncomfortable to do. With that in mind, there are situations, although not many, that could benefit from having an individual without a conscience. Although they would sacrifice one person in order to save a large group, their inner motive would lead them to only save themselves.

Claiming that a disorder is desirable for society is a clever way to effortlessly brush the problem aside and ignore any chance of treatment. Asserting that psychopaths help solve problems ignores the fact that problems improve faster without any malfunctioning individual involved. If a business needs someone that is willing to put themselves on the line and perform their uncomfortable tasks, they can instill those ideals into their employees without the utilization of a disorder. Nevertheless, since these individuals are almost always present in workplace environments, one is left with the opportunity to strive to employ their behavior to the best of our ability. In other words, one can be left with the shocking reality that these individuals do no less than surround them in day-today life. Decade after decade, these individuals are groomed into people that are harmful, at best. In an ideal scenario, they would function to their best capacity, in order to improve their environment. Unfortunately, the opposite is done—they hide their disorder and use it for their own personal profit. This present-day layout is not ideal. Although, society does not yet have the knowledge to know how to handle and coach these individuals into being helpful towards society. Therefore, society must attempt to learn more, and acknowledge the fact that it is unwise to assume ASPD as profitable within the human species. Not only does this paint an inaccurate picture of personality disorders, but disregards the entirety of the burden it places on all of those affected as well.

CHAPTER FOUR – A GLIMPSE INTO THE LIFE OF THOSE WITH ASPD

Those who are against the "medicalising" of antisocial behavior do not have the disorder themselves. Although the word "diagnosis" carries along with it a negative connotation, the recognition of Antisocial Personality Disorder is the first step to understanding that individual's behavior, motives, as well as marks the first step towards potential treatment. That being said, a quick web search of this disorder will bring one to believe, within minutes, that the affected individual is dangerous and violent, to say the least. While low functioning individuals with ASPD are prone to committing violent acts against others, the majority do not. Yet, the media continues to portray them as threats, allowing society to view them as just that as well. Threat or not, it is important to understand, or at the least, try to understand, what made each individual into the way that they are. It is the belief that some can be genetically predisposed to ASPD. This predisposition, mixed with a harmful childhood environment, creates a lethal combination. Some with ASPD look back on their childhood and have no recollection of attaching emotions to any memories whatsoever. They replay vivid moments from their past yet see them neutrally, no matter the actual event. Most of the time, the individual is aware, from a young age, that they are different from the rest. While other kids cry and get upset, they watch and can't seem to relate to such a reaction. Without a diagnosis, these individuals will remain confused about their mental standing—as well as continue to manifest the appropriate reaction while remaining neutral inside, every single time.

These individuals do not have a clear path of what they envision their life to end up like because they have no preference. Even as they age, they will attempt to create their life on what seems to be the correct road, since they have no other map to build off of besides the persistent social observation of others. Since their boredom never subsides, no job will ever satisfy them. While one has specific passions and hobbies that they can can immerse themselves into at any given time, the "psychopath" has no real way to ever cure their offset mind. Treatment will, one day, be able to evoke some sort of emotional response within the individual. Right now, the medication treatment does nothing but dull their senses even further while continually ignoring the remaining question: the cause of the disorder. Without a diagnosis, the individual will continue to live their double life, promoting the destruction of others without any knowledge on how to stop it, or even more dangerous, what created it in the first place.

The majority of studies on ASPD continue to be done on those individuals already involved in the criminal justice system. These studies send the message to the average individual with ASPD that they remain perpetually misunderstood, since their only representation within the population exists in correctional settings involving punishment. This not only evokes a feeling of being misunderstood, but vulnerability, since the consequences of being open about one's ASPD are widely unknown.

Whether one has empathy for the "psychopath" is up to them. What is not up for debate, however, is the reality that they cannot control their behavior. They act in the hopes that others pity them, and although they may not be deserving of pity, help, along with any amount of empathy, has the potential to go a long way and serve a purpose. The amount of effort that these individuals put into their lives often goes unnoticed. For them, otherwise routine actions become strategic acts. These individuals are malfunctioning, and their mindset makes if awfully difficult to appear normal. An immense amount of mental labor goes into the construction of their image. They persistently have two contrasting, distinct selves at work, battling each other on how to act or what choices to make. While the outer image appears calm, interested and often intelligent, the inner self struggles to find the desired route of action. This inner self puts intense work into building the outer image—trying to make him appear as normal as possible, feeding each individual the unique reaction that they are believed to desire. The individual he interacts with becomes the guide for the choices he will make. He often mirrors their behavior, as well as predicts their reactions. Over time, he will master this skill through the watchful examination of others. They are deception in the flesh, made of a carefully crafted self exhibited to the world, and a separate self that is strategically tucked away, always mindful of the next step in order to arrive at the following goal. No work of art and no place on earth have the capability to spark an emotional reaction out of him. He does not experience fight or flight, the same way that most of us do. Nothing initiates fear. Nothing is out of bounds for him. The way that these individuals take care of their timeless boredom is through the manipulation of their chosen target. Even *while* they have the target in the palm of their hand, they are plotting their next victim.

In order to reach their goal, they become skilled at forecasting the reactions of their targets. A large sum of their work is accurately being able to tell whether or not the other individual will give into their schemes. In order to anticipate the next move, they envision themselves in the worlds of their targets, since they do not possess any emotional experiences of their own to go off of. While placing themselves into the world of the target's, they often end up unable to leave their own characteristics in their own life, and instead apply them to the target. For instance, it is said that if the individual with ASPD feels aggressive, they imagine their target as more aggressive than they truly are, despite any evidence that might prove them wrong. Not only aggressiveness, but many of the sociopath/psychopath's own traits are carelessly thrown onto their perception of how their target is. Their view is distorted, since they have no personal knowledge of what being a neurotypical is truly like.

Again and again, it is the good-natured individuals that are taken under the manipulation process and discarded much worse off than before. The undertaking of recovery is an extensive affair. Once left in the dust, these individuals are frequently left asking questions about why the other individual left such a mark on their well-being. The answer being: Antisocial Personality Disorder.

CHAPTER FIVE – HOW THOSE WITH ASPD CHOOSE TARGETS

For someone with ASPD, it is all about control. This makes sense, keeping in mind that they view life as a game, and human beings as objects. They do not see people as functional members of society. They do not believe that anyone has a right to individuality. Instead, they view each person as a tool to be used towards their own benefit.

When this person first discovers a viable target, they glorify that person until they are placed on their hierarchy… above all of their previous targets. They attempt to find out everything about that person. Thus, in trivial conversations, they will not do most of the talking. They study that person's fears, hobbies, and even go so far as adopt their interests as their own. At some point in the future, this information will be used against their target effectively. They make sure that their target knows that they are in high demand— they aren't the only person obsessed with them. Still, they decided to make the target first place on their list. They convince the target that they are special by quickly declaring a rare, soul-mate connection. Yet, not after long, that same target "slips out of first place" while trying to do everything to remain their soul-mate. The psychopath will reach out to old targets while simultaneously seeking out new ones, causing their current victim to become more and more desperate to keep their place in their life. The target will do anything. They begin to act needy and clingy, pushing the psychopath even further away.

They condition their targets to believe that their abuse is not the problem, but rather their very reactions to their abuse. One of their main goals is to turn their targets against themselves in order to effectively distract them from noticing their destructive behavior towards them. They will predict the target's reactions and be prepared to invalidate anything they say. Further on in a relationship with this type of individual, one will begin to doubt themselves more as time goes on. When confronting these individuals with a problem, they will provide their target with a muddled and lengthy response, avoiding the actual concern all together. The target is often left wondering if their problem was even addressed. Very quickly, and devastatingly, doubt sets into the target and they begin to question their own beliefs. They begin to view the psychopath as a perfect individual whose "personality" unfortunately no longer seems to match up with their consistent abusive behavior. Unfortunately, it is impossible for any type of relationship to have meaning for these individuals. They will terminate the relationship when it suits best for them, no matter how deep into it they have gone. They are skilled at figuring out other's deepest characteristics and using the flaws towards their own benefit. They view the downfall of their targets as beneficial toward their uprising. They know what they are doing is wrong, which is why they go through so much trouble to mask the behavior. Covert abuse is hard to detect, the tactics are relatively unknown. To begin clearly, covert abuse includes any deceitful, underhanded behavior on the part of the abuser used to manipulate others in order to gain power and control. While physical and verbal abuse are easy to point out, in most cases, covert abuse is never simple. It is likely that the victim will not identify any abuse until long after the relationship is done for. The victim will not realize they are being manipulated, which is why they begin to question their own sanity instead of the perpetrator's. By the time they identify any type of abuse, the individual with ASPD has successfully eradicated their support system, leaving them with nobody left to even believe that they have been abused in the first place. From an outsider's view, the "psychopath" will remain calm, cool and collected, while the victim seems to have entered the realms of insanity, doing anything to grasp their sense of reality once again.

Some may do research about "psychopaths" and immediately attribute their characteristics to someone they know, instantly questioning whether or not their peers have Antisocial Personality Disorder. The main difference between these individuals and their acquaintances is their strategic covert abuse. They idealize and groom their targets. This is why they are so hard to spot, since they present themselves as if they were a normal person. Based on their findings in regards to who their target is, they manifest themselves into their mirror image, making their targets that much more attached. One must be able to recognize a 50/50 relationship, a two-sided relationship, over one where the other person is the hostage of another. They craft themselves into you for a reason. It is not the rules created within our society that cause one to behave morally, it is their conscience.

Not only is their covert abuse hard to recognize, their trauma bonding as well. The victim develops an attachment to the "psychopath" that seems unbreakable in the beginning stages. Within no time, the victim relies on the individual to meet their basic needs and supply their own happiness. In an obviously abusive relationship, the clear solution would be abandoning the abuser. While this may seem simple to an outsider, relationships with "sociopaths" or "psychopaths" involve covert abuse, and these individuals utilize intermittent reinforcement to prevent the victim from leaving, every time their mind urges them to do so. They are said to "drag their victims through a cycle of punishments and rewards," and every time the victim want to leave, they'll give them a reason to stay. Every interaction will be strategic, with the target's reaction as the predicted and desired result. They will make any lie, no matter how unbelievable, seem true by inserting parts of the truth.

While they seem to have power over their victims, the underlying reason for their manipulative behavior is their own lacking in an understanding of life. They have no real navigational skills or connection to reality. They have no knowledge of any social skills that get them what they want without the use of manipulation or lies. They manufacture their arguments in such a way that it would be impossible for them to lose. If they cannot find an answer for the question that has been posed to them, they will distract with other elements of the truth and leave the victim more confused than before the entire conversation. They will switch the focus from their behavior to their target's obsessiveness. If the conversation ever shifts back to them, they will attempt to evoke pity in their victim. They will do anything to ensure that their behavior is never addressed.

Triangulation is one of the most common manipulation tactics utilized by the psychopath. To define it simply, triangulation is when one person doesn't communicate directly with another person, and instead uses a third person to relay certain messages to the second, thus forming a triangle. This is how the psychopath turns their previous, current, and future targets against each other throughout this system of relaying strategic messages. Through triangulation, they will make the current victim compete with their new and old targets, making themselves seem on high demand while simultaneously turning the current target against their "crazy" exes. On the outside, this spread of gossip/information can be deemed meaningless, yet the reality is that their goal is to make their target eventually confront them about their actions. Since they seem mundane and routine, this confrontation will paint their target as the crazy and dramatic one, thus fulfilling their ultimate goal. While this target knows, intuitively, that their "small" actions are meant to cause a riot within them, it will be impossible to prove to an outside party—which the perpetrator is highly aware of. The psychopath alters their victims' opinions by convincing them that their past exes were crazy. They will quickly turn the current target against everyone from their past, making them resent anyone who has "hurt" their new partner, the psychopath. Yet, when their time is up and the supply has been put to use, the new target will come to resent the current one as well. This type of manipulation, triangulation, marks the beginning of what some refer to as the "smear campaign"—their plot to discredit their victims and paint them as insane, despite lack of concrete evidence. The last stage in their plot of triangulation occurs when they decide to let the current target go, claiming that they have hurt them and that the target possesses a behavior that has been toxic within their lives. While they put the blame onto their victim, they will have been ignoring all of their efforts to save the relationship, setting aside any attempts that have been made to remain on good terms. The victim will remain confused as to why the psychopath refuses to address any of these problems, since, at this point, the problems are what make up the entire relationship.

Before they let go of the current victim, they will have secured their new target to take their place. They will make their target believe that the ending of the relationship is due to their obsessive behavior, while simultaneously using their downfall to show the new target that they are on high demand, and so loved by everybody, yet, they decided to choose them. Since, as we have gone over, they have become so skilled at predicting the reactions of others, the end of the relationship consists of them using those very reactions to prove to others that their target *is* the crazy person that they have made them out to be.

Those who come across a psychopath do not know what to make of them. All they know is that they strive for their approval, for whatever reason. They are clingy towards anyone who shows a potential supply towards their benefit, and show their affection through non-stop texting and flattering comments on social media. This is ironic, since later on, the target becomes the clingy one. Almost immediately, their victims become reliant on their communication as a source of confidence. They will declare a soul-mate connection rather quickly, and although the target may not be able to put your finger on the reasoning, not many targets find their declarations of love creepy. Many targets rapidly find out that they seem to have a lot in common with this person, since they do most of the talking while they manifest into the mirror image of that. They put the current target on a pedestal by comparing them to their past "toxic" exes, yet later on end up tearing them down by choosing those same exes over the current target.

The target will label their covertly abusive behavior as accidental, since there's a race between them and their other targets to keep their appraisal. Although the targets are in constant competition for this individual's attention, they don't seem to give much thought to what they do. Once they notice that the targets are hooked, they suddenly become apathetic and distant, ensuring that each target is the one needing to initiate contact. When their victims try to express themselves truthfully, they will give a condescending smirk, and tease with insults disguised as jokes. The victims seem to be the only one that notices this type of behavior. While they desperately try to convince others to view this person in the same light, they remain loyal in admiring them. These people, the psychopath's acquaintances, will be used for money, attention, and other resources to feed towards their spotless reputation. They will be blind to the fact that they are being used all together, since the psychopathic individual will praise them intermittently. These individuals make up their friendships, since the psychopath is not capable of keeping a stable, deep friendship, but rather many mere acquaintances all together.

When their mask comes off, their behavior will drastically change, since they cater their behavior to whomever they are around at the time. They adopt different personalities to act as the mirror image of the target they are interacting with at the time, almost transforming themselves within each various interaction. They jump into each relationship extremely fast, locking in their targets quickly, before any manipulation can be clearly identified. Ironically, while they will seem so similar to their target, that same target ends up rooting them on so much that they forget their own lives in the process. The life that they are now supporting involves overlapping relationships, failed connections, and lack of any real nostalgia in relationship to the past.

Do you know who the best manipulators are? Exactly. Their public image is often higher than perfect, and it is not a coincidence. That's why the victims become so dumbfounded by their behavior. They will do things like contact their targets and then claim that the text was made for someone else. They will set out false concern, for example, hope that the other person feels better if they are ill. They will act cowardly, and rely on third parties to contact you in order to keep tabs—triangulation. If they do not receive their desired response, it will be flipped onto the victim. They'll ask why they have been contacted in the first place, even if they were the ones who initiated the contact. They will find mundane ways to keep in touch with you, making them seem urgent while trying to hold onto the emotional supply of the victim by a single thread.

As far as discarding goes, common discarding situations include catastrophes, and paradoxically, holidays. If a cherished love one passes away or someone becomes increasingly sick, they will get rid them since they no longer pose any use. On the contrary, holidays provide them a perfect moment to ruin, thus why they love discarding when the victim least expects it, or when everything else seems to be going well. Without realizing it, many victims are afraid to heal because that means letting go of their life with the perpetrator. With time, they will begin to question how their insanity began to manifest without them being conscious of it. It must be taken note of that targets who are confused shall never think of themselves as the one to blame. Victims are not weak, but merely kind hearted people in the wrong place at the wrong time. Although the victim will want to go around town defending themselves, this will only prove the sociopath correct in how they have branded them. The image of their victim has been publicized in advance, and they have anticipated their reactions. The target will end up shocked and confused, but understanding the mental state of these individuals is crucial to understanding the fact that the victims could not have known.

After the discard, they will feel incredibly superior while watching their victim's developing confusion. During this time period, they become increasingly calm in order to amplify any emotions that the victim evokes within their (normal) reaction to the abuse. They'll speak down to their victim and be more than casual, avoiding any talk about their own lies while the victim glorifies them in their memory as they walk away.

While a standard breakup is hard enough, these individuals make sure to leave at the most unexpected time. They do not care about an explanation, yet later they will attempt to gain access to their previous targets yet again.

Many believe in the idea that no contact involves forcing oneself away from their perpetrator while maintaining the toxic emotional attachment. Yet, it turns out that detached contact is about remaining emotionally distant, even *while* in the presence of someone toxic.

It is important to take note that their "new supply" is not an upgrade, but simply a new source of energy towards their eternal boredom. Although this leaves the former victim desperate and searching for answers, the answers they expect will never come, because the reality does not match up to the situation that has been put in the victim's mind. As the victim's supply for the sociopath begins to run out, they become more and more bored, on the prowl for their next target. They begin to change rapidly and engage in erratic behavior, since they now only have to mirror the behavior of their new target and no longer any current victim. Their current target's behavior is the only conscience they have to work off of. If their own behavior is questioned, the discarding period comes even more rapidly than before in their attempt to escape any questions or doubts about their newfound confusing demeanor. The only way to win the game is to not play.

The search for the silver lining in a relationship with a sociopath may not yield great results, yet, they can be discovered. The original misconceptions that one has against someone with ASPD can teach them what they want in a relationship. Paradoxically, the person they turn out to be can teach them what they do not want. And one who believes that a relationship with a sociopath is worth trying to recover must keep in mind that someone with ASPD almost always involves abuse. None of their actions will ever involve remorse, and crime is inevitable in many of the situations regarding Antisocial Personality Disorder, whether that be criminal activity or emotional abuse/covert manipulation.

Those who are empaths and idealists, although seemingly possess admirable qualities, have somewhat of a curse. While many spend their youth doubting their own intuition and striving to please others, their journey later on ends in no longer getting joy from their normal habits. Toxic relationships make them doubt themselves more than their perpetrators and their unmatchable behavior. In the beginning, these doubts send them on a path that convinces them they will no longer have joy again. Yet, ultimately, it sends them on an expedition to discover more: motives, deeper meanings, and wisdom. The perpetrator, on the other hand, may never escape the suffering of their mental state, unlike the victim who will reach a higher level of understanding.

CHAPTER SIX – THE DIAGNOSIS OF A PERSONALITY DISORDER

The center of attention must shift away from criminal activity and closer towards personality traits. Criminal activity does not call for the assumption that the criminal has ASPD. In fact, the dyssocial sociopath was removed from the DSM for this very reason. The dyssocial sociopath, in the old DSM, was defined as someone who could be loyal to their fellow comrades, such as, those in organized crime. This leaves one with nothing but the description of an individual who *does* possess the capacity to maintain long relationships and form real bonds with others. All that one has left to go off of, in this case, to warrant a diagnosis of ASPD, is the mere engagement in criminal activity. This does not, as previously discussed, warrant a diagnosis. A finding of criminal activity within one's history is insignificant in relation to Antisocial Personality

Disorder. The majority of crimes are carried out by psychopaths. There is, though, a psychopathic personality that never makes contact with the criminal justice system, and because of that, never gets a diagnosis of ASPD. There is also a psychopathic personality that does interact with the criminal justice system, and because of that, ends up being diagnosed with the disorder. The differences of these two personalities must be highlighted, and deserve more investigation as a whole. Although the debate on what makes one a psychopath has yet to end, the impact of their behavior has remained uniform throughout history. For those affected, it is of great significance that these individuals are diagnosed fairly.

Many forensic professionals still have doubt about the line between psychopathy and ASPD. In the most current version of the DSM, the terms sociopathy/psychopathy are outdated, leaving one with only the term Antisocial Personality Disorder. Within the realm of ASPD, many psychologists have asserted that sociopaths and psychopaths are one in the same and the terms can, thus, be used interchangeably. It is also a widespread belief that most individuals who have ASPD are not psychopaths, however, most psychopaths *do* end up becoming involved in antisocial behaviors. It has also been theorized that the sociopath is created, and the psychopath is born. For generations, this has been the main, defining difference between the two without question. With all of this in mind, it is imperative to note that criminal behavior alone is insignificant, and does not mean that one has ASPD or is a psychopath.

Not only for those affected, but for the individuals themselves, it is crucial that the diagnostic line between ASPD and psychopathy is made more clear. Often, the two are not distinct from one another, even in hazardous times. Concerns about countertransference have continued to be expressed as well—while the professionals controlling the diagnosis lean towards actually wanting to diagnose one with ASPD towards their advantage. One may wish to diagnose the criminal with ASPD in order to benefit the situation. Bail is based on how much risk one will continue to pose. But a diagnosis must never be done out of self-interest. The fundamental troubles after a diagnosis of psychopathy are more severe than that of any other mental illness, since those with ASPD almost always undergo punishment after experiencing the extreme vulnerability of exposing their disorder. The fate of these individuals is dependent on the forensic department's understanding of their disorder. The fate of the criminal as a whole must be taken care of, and just because someone has a recurring pattern of criminal activity does not mean that they also have the inability to create attachments or change their behavior in the future.

When attempting to diagnose, or rule out a diagnosis, the professional is likely to hear exactly what they want to hear. The individual, if they do in fact have ASPD, is extremely skilled at displaying the socially appropriate emotion at the correct time. This is why face value behaviors do not provide enough evidence for a diagnosis. Instead, they must be questioned further, versus being merely observed. "He knows the words to the song, but he can't hear the music", is often used to describe how the sociopath/psychopath understands the emotions of others. Although they will exhibit the desired reaction, they do not inherently know how it feels to truly have that reaction. For one case, the individual may say they feel guilty. However, it would be in good nature for the professional to then inquire further about how it felt to feel guilt. Suddenly, the individual will become confused and flustered. They know that guilt was the correct emotion, but if they are unable to experience it, they will not know how it feels, let alone how to describe that feeling.

As established as early as 1997, the four standards for civil confinement include: a current mental disorder or abnormality, a strong potential to commit sexual crimes in the future, a history of sexual violence or a mental abnormality that is likely to lead to new sexual offenses. If one chooses to take a diagnosis of ASPD, or any mental abnormality, lightly, they must remember that release is contingent on improvement. Right now, in order to qualify for a diagnosis of ASPD, at least four of ten behaviors must be met: inability to sustain consistent work behavior, impulsive conduct, inability to establish lasting and stable relationships, irritable and aggressive, lying, indicated by physical fights or assaults, and disregard for personal safety, as stated by the APA in 1987.

The movement away from sociopathy/psychopathy and towards Antisocial Personality Disorder has had many professionals contemplating what truly makes up a diagnosis. Many believe that different levels of ASPD can be seen, depending on the individual, and the amount of peril actually varies from person to person. This is where the PCL-R scale comes in. As defined in The Encyclopedia of Mental Disorders, The Hare Pyschopathy Checklist is a diagnostic tool that rates a person's psychopathic or antisocial tendencies. Specifically, it measures the degree to which the person has these tendencies. This test has been previously used in mental facilities, prisons, and is awaiting approval to be put to use in correctional facilities, as well as more criminal cases regarding sex offenders, specifically.

In recent years, many professionals have been urgent to put the PCL-R scale to use. This psychopathy-checklist is more popular since it does not rely too much on behaviors, and does not neglect the importance of one's personality traits. Previous criteria relied on behavior, and sacrificed validity for reliability. In other words, it was unknown how accurate the measures were, even though they were consistent. These were the issues that prompted Hare to create his Psychopathy Checklist in the first place. The test has good norms, reliability and validity, according to Hare in 1991. The test views psychopathy from a two-factor perspective, with 20 characteristics total. 17 out of 20 of the characteristics fall under one of the two factors. According to Meloy in 1998, Factor

1 represents "aggressive narcissism" and addresses emotional/interactional social styles. It measures personality traits such as superficial charm, glibness, pathological lying, shallow affect, etc. Factor 2, on the other hand, addresses the behavioral aspects that are common in psychopaths. To mention a few: proneness to boredom, lack of realistic long-term goals, and a parasitic lifestyle. As one gets older, Factor 2 items may diminish with age, according to Hare. However, Factor 1 items tend to remain constant over the course of one's lifetime.

In regards to criminology, one can conclude that static factors determine levels of future harm that one may pose, while dynamic factors are used to predict the likelihood of harm posed to the community in the years to come after release. A diagnosis of ASPD alone decides whether or not one is qualified for future treatment. With that in action, an individual with a diagnosis of ASPD (due to their behavior) may be falsely labeled as someone who is untreatable.

The Sexually Violent Predator Act in 1995 states that SVPs generally have antisocial characteristics that do not allow them to receive any mental illness treatments, since their pre-existing antisocial personality features are likely to cause them to continue to engage in sexually violent behavior. To this day, it is unclear whether they were speaking on ASPD or psychopathy, which is why the distinction must be made, especially in legal cases like these. This act was upheld, and many forensic psychologists claim that its goal was to keep the offender held for life. It does so by labeling the offender as a psychopath, or as one with ASPD. This effectively warrants that a release is highly unlikely, since improvement is seen as impossible within these offenders.

While the detection of either psychopathy or ASPD is forlorn for the culprit, the aftermath is much darker. This is why the professional must question their client further—not just about the emotions they claim to have experienced, but how it felt to experience them as well. Their sentence, as well as their release, is contingent on the probability of their improvement to come. This is why all declarations of mental illnesses are, to say the least, significant events in the lives of those at hand.

CHAPTER SEVEN – THE CAUSES OF ANTISOCIAL PERSONALITY DISORDER

Humans follow what they see. The behavior that is modeled during one's youth later manifests itself into the groundwork that the individual will later live by. Victims of abuse are shown that experiences of power are valuable, and only gained through the powerless experience of the victim. This demonstration of behavior modeling turns the victim into an abuser. Ironically, those who turn out to be abusers often brand themselves as the victim in any viable situation. Often times, they brand themselves as the victim in order to effectively dismiss their own reckless behavior. In cases of emotional abuse, it is hard to detect any evidence that proves that the victim is undergoing mistreatment. Yet, one will find that treatment brings dramatic, positive changes to the emotional stability of the individual who was previously abused.

The process in which the abused become the abusers can be seen in how they treat others. Often times, they have automatic defense systems that involve expecting to be mistreated, thus, these situations often end in them inflicting the ill treatment onto others first. Abusers frequently become angry if they are not immediately branded as the victim in any given situation. In order to avoid this, these individuals will try to justify their behavior through any means possible. They induce shame onto their victims, claim that they are the ones undergoing abuse, or reinforce their sense of entitlement by engaging in self-righteous behavior.

A psychopath is a psychopath is a psychopath. But is that the truth? The way that one's personality forms is the direct result of how they believe they should act within their community, as well as how they have adapted within society over the course of their life. This all depends on how their community views certain behavior. Personality disorders reflect this part of the developmental process. Psychopathy and different levels of ASPD as a whole have been found to vary from one individual compared to the next. This has raised several questions about the causes of psychopaths/sociopaths and ASPD. Are these individuals products of environmental circumstances? More importantly, and closer to home, one must ask begin to ask themselves and inquire further: what about our culture, here, promotes the common behaviors exhibited from these individuals? Are these just normal people branded into psychopaths? At the end of the day, what makes someone a psychopath? As it turns out, culture has an impact. Studies have shown that individuals who have ASPD each show it in a different way, despite the fact that they each have ASPD. One study found that callousness was the main behavior in US-based offenders, while the predominant behavior in Dutch offenders was irresponsibility. The way that ASPD can be seen varies throughout different cultures. With this in mind, one can infer that culture promotes, as well as scolds, certain behavioral patterns, thus shaping the way that a psychopath learns to act within their community.

It has been said that personality disorders are a product of genetics, critical early experiences and social environment. This means that financial status, living conditions, and attachment to parents all have the potential to influence the development of ASPD. Within these factors are a handful of cultural influences, and the way that an individual is raised in one culture will be very different from that of another. Our universal definition of ASPD, as well as our mental image of a "psychopath", can be thrown out the window when comparing these varying cultures and their behavioral ideals.

The impact of culture on one's personality development can be seen within their behaviors later on in life. American culture, in particular, has been said to actually encourage the manifestation of this disorder. The values of Western entities are what influence the creation of ASPD. Whether this be unconscious or intentional, it can be seen in America's leaders, media and much more. The patriarchy promotes toxic masculinity, and the nation as a whole pushes individualism onto all of its members. From an extremely young age, boys are raised to become dominant and assertive. American society places men on the competitive plane. Competition is branded deep within them from the point of their upbringing, and for the rest of their lives. Without sufficient reason, they are seen within the images of success more commonly than women are. This is the precise image that the American culture thoughtlessly promotes. Anything feminine, on the contrary, is seen as lower and less functional than masculinity. Even men together are raised to point out the feminine traits of their peers and identify them as flaws. This is the backbone of an environment that instills Antisocial Personality Disorder into children from a young age.

If there remains any speculation about whether or not American culture promotes Antisocial Personality Disorder, further evidence can be brought to the surface. Haung and Tang have found that the rate of personality disorders in China is far lower than Western countries. This is because, as mentioned before, different cultures idealize different personality traits. After all, the way that a person behaves is dependent on how they were taught to behave. This all goes back to the standards of one's culture—what is seen as harmful in one culture may be helpful in another. Michie and Cooke have claimed that abnormal behaviors and the promotion of individualism/collectivism are correlated. They argue that collectivistic cultures, where the well-being of the community is a top priority, have lower crime rates than individualistic societies, like Western cultures. Looking further, it can be seen that collectivistic societies promote the social good, while individualistic societies function on the competitive plane. One gets what they want, in Western culture, through inconsiderateness and competition. Many are built to have a strong competitive drive. This is a strong factor that can easily lead to manipulative behavior and lack of emotion. Competitiveness promotes the worsening of others while cooperativeness promotes the wellness of others.

If it can be acknowledged the reality that culture, as well as the factors that make up one's upbringing, encourage the behaviors of ASPD, it can also be noted, with extreme hopefulness and confidence, that there exists great reason to believe that these behaviors are preventable. The more that one culture understands mental illness, the more effective that the culture can be in preventing the development of those illnesses. Cultural relativism claims that culture has the greatest impact on personality development, while cultural psychology asserts that culture and personality mutually influence each other. In either sense, it would be logical to conclude that culture has the potential to act as a deciding factor in regards to whether or not one ends up with ASPD, or, in any case, other disorders.

CHAPTER EIGHT – THE UNSPOKEN PROBLEMS OF ASPD

Many advances have been made in eradicating stigmas, from topics like mental health to homosexuality. Organizations like NAMI, The Gay & Lesbian Leadership Institute and many more have raised awareness and formed accepting beliefs into the minds of those who speak on these sensitive topics. The first step to eradicating any stigma is the general education involving the topic at hand. Therefore, when dealing with mental illnesses, one must never underestimate the overwhelming power, although it deems itself simple, of education.

Although there does exist extensive research in an attempt to explore the views of those with Antisocial Personality Disorder, few have succeeded in providing accurate depictions. In low security environments, the individual has gone very far in their lives without disclosing much in regards to their disorder, and is almost impossible to interview. In high risk environments, such as correctional facilities, the individuals are not willing to expose their own point of view due to the fact that it provides no further benefit for them. In 2000 a study was conducted to interview those with ASPD in regards to what it felt like to be diagnosed. 22% of the participants in the study claimed that a diagnosis of Antisocial Personality Disorder is "a label you get when 'they' don't know what else to do with you". 10% of the participants related their diagnosis to something 'bad' and 'untreatable'. It is not uncommon that the individual feels neglected by healthcare professionals. Once the diagnosis is complete, many feel isolated and confused as to where they belong, as well as fearful toward what the next steps might be. Those with a diagnosis of ASPD may be treated as if they do not have a mental illness, but a disorder that they have brought upon themselves. In a handful of cases, ASPD is taken less seriously than other disorders. The services that are provided for those with personality disorders may not be as well equipped to deal with Antisocial Personality Disorder, specifically, due to the fact that they are not specialized. Furthermore, many services often exclude those with ASPD over other mental disorders that seem to grant more hope or potential for improvement. In regards to ASPD in itself, the amount of understanding and empathy is not provided due to the ongoing stigma. From the POV of a diagnosed individual, it is not far-fetched to assume that one would predict future punishment more often than future treatment options.

On a general level, the term 'personality disorder' has not left many of the affected unsatisfied. Although it may be discouraging to experience a diagnosis, the term 'personality disorder' in itself does not have the negative connotation attached. This goes to show that it is Antisocial Personality Disorder by itself that gives the notion of hopelessness. To build further, those with Borderline Personality Disorder, in various studies, have spoken in positive fashion about their experiences with their healthcare professionals. It is not personality disorders themselves that grant labels of dismissiveness and mistreatment, but the infamous reputation of ASPD on its own that has deemed itself not worth dealing with. Yet, this same reputation also grants more research and effort, proving that it warrants even further investigation than those disorders that have already made this progress. The more hopeless that one sees ASPD, the more urgent the very issue becomes.

Although ASPD is a conclusive diagnosis placed on the affected individuals, many of them are quite different in regards to their inner thoughts and behavior. Although their personalities are malfunctioning, and in some cases, severely so... each individual's experience with their personality disorder is unique. This is why the focus on the individual is extremely important, and not merely the diagnosis alone.

In a study conducted by Castillo and colleagues in 2001, participants with any type of personality disorder (predominantly Borderline) had experienced childhood abuse. Specifically, out of the 50 participants, 88% had experienced some type of abuse, with the majority taking place during their childhood years. This early abuse is thought to be the cause of a malfunctioning personality later on in life. In regards to the women with personality disorders, every single one in Castillo's study had experienced childhood emotional abuse. Yet, while none had a history of being violent as a child, 67% had grown up to become violent. Many within this study have claimed to have been told that they are a not worth the help—a lost cause. In other studies, participants being unable to form and maintain relationships with others is not an uncommon theme. This is the coping strategy being put to use—the after effects of prior abuse can be seen on the forefront.

Common strategies to counteract adapted detrimental coping mechanisms include visiting mental health centers, talking to a professional and simply keeping active. Often times, those with personality disorders, on a general level, engage in harmful behavior such as self harm or over-medication. The healthier alternatives, however, are seldom recognized or publicized. These grant further recognition due to the fact that they are so accessible and easy to publicize for those dealing with personality disorders. If one does not have access to treatment, simple coping skills and healthy activities shall be let out to the public in order to help aid those with personality disorders who are looking to change their ways, which, is far more than many would expect. Whether one's goal is to seem more reliable towards the public or to prevent future destruction, many coping mechanisms on how to cure boredom can be noted.

Although a diagnosis of ASPD carries with it the label of helplessness that always seems to be tied on, the individual can use this discovery to better understand the reasons behind their actions. Their life, for themselves and others, will make a great deal of sense after a diagnosis. Not only that, but the individual can learn how to function like normal within society, versus the life prior to the diagnosis of not knowing what the problem was, and not knowing how to fix it. Even after a diagnosis of ASPD, the journey to functioning normal within a community is never straightforward or easy. However, after pondering and putting to use the best ways to function/cope, it would be shocking to see one with ASPD being viewed as abnormal by their peers. Yet, on the inner foreground, eternal boredom will sink in. On the visible side, now speaking, we can see the eternal boredom set in when the need for stimulation produces needless actions. That is why coping mechanisms are worth being put to use… engaging in healthy activities, will allow the functioning of a helpful member in society overcome any need to fill the lack of stimulation. It would not be appalling for someone to suggest that those with ASPD look in speechless wonder at those who function normally. These individuals may be eternally curious about how others live life so present in the moment and emotional. Yet, they do not know.

In regards to the caretakers of those with ASPD, one common theme that has been discovered is caretakers feeling that they lack the knowledge or skills to keep an eye on one with a personality disorder. The lack of training within the department of health to care for those with personality disorders is visibly lacking. This can, devastatingly, often be seen in situations where the caretaker wants to lash out or give up on the individual.

Interestingly, in a study conducted by Mercer and colleagues in 2000, forensic nurses' attitudes towards ASPD were revealed. When discussing perpetrators of violent crimes, many nurses labeled the patients as 'evil' and 'beyond the scope of treatment' in regards to their severe Antisocial Personality Disorder. On the contrary, patients experiencing psychosis or schizophrenia were granted the opportunity to be understood by their staff. In areas of attempted treatment, 'therapeutic pessimism' is a common term to describe the relationship between client and professional. Due to the sense of hopelessness and evil commonly tied to ASPD, negative attitudes ensue throughout any process of counseling. One way to counteract this negativity is to train staff on how to handle patients with personality disorders, specifically. This will open their eyes to the possibility that treatment, or improvement, is on the rise and plausible. In the training of staff, one should take note of the potential effectiveness that an emphasis on individuality can have. To look into this deeper… a professional who views each patient as a complex individual, and who attempts to form an effective professional/beneficial bond with each of them, would render far more productive than one who views all patients with ASPD as the same collective person. The value of caring about the patient, although incredibly simple, is often understated in regards to personality disorders. Not only that, but the labels placed around ASPD, and personality disorders as a whole, are, to say the least, counterproductive. Recognizing that each individual (although they are people of the same disorder) possess their own needs will be the first building block towards effective treatment for each, and eventually, all.

Group sessions, in regards to patients as well as staff, may be proven effective in easing the difficult emotions that arise in correctional facilities or mental institutions. For instance, Grendon Underwood Prison has developed staff sensitivity groups in which their goal is to discuss and deal with the emotional problems that arise from dealing with patients who have personality disorders. Not only staff, but patients themselves can greatly benefit from this type of group work/group therapy. Those with personality disorders, although each possess their individual needs, could benefit from group work and feel less isolated by the end of the discussion activities.

In staff interviewed in 2007 by Huband and Duggan, many members reported undergoing basic training in regards to dealing with patients with personality disorders. Interestingly, these same staff members claimed to know little about personality disorders themselves. Data like this can reveal the root of the problem in regards to caretaking—the caretakers are more often than not under educated, as well as the general public in regards to personality disorders. Many effective potential strategies have been identified, but are not yet being put to use. For instance, in a study conducted by Crawford and Rutter, staff suggested focusing on situation-specific training as well as general training in regards to learning more about ASPD and personality disorders as a whole. Open discussion about how to handle individuals with ASPD can improve staff dynamics as a whole, make sure that the entire staff is on the same page when taking care of these individuals.

CHAPTER NINE – THE HISTORY OF ANTISOCIAL PERSONALITY DISORDER TREATMENT

The 1959 Mental Health Act, as stated in its legislation, sought to remove the distinction between psychiatric hospitals and hospitals in general. This was a groundbreaking and radical movement, encouraging equality between mental and physical health services. The act also increased optimism among the general public, not only in regards to personality disorders, but mental health issues as a whole. Before this act, high security environments were the closest thing to treatment for those struggling with ASPD. This took place in the post-war period, while psychiatry was seemingly increasing its value and being put to use more often due to the prevalence of mental disorders, like PTSD, increasing. Not only was there an increase in the psychoanalysis of patients, but there was an increase in the belief that an environment *can* cause certain mental deficiencies, as well as the belief that an environment can be a means of treating them. Many therapies began to focus on problems within one's personality, versus the prior notion that personality disorders were hopeless, and that permanent problems would remain throughout the patient's lifetime with no prevail.

To the public's surprise, many of the first effective therapeutic communities began in correctional facilities, focusing on issues like drug and alcohol problems. These sectors nailed in on a focus of the patient's interpersonal and social difficulties, as well as each individual's specific needs, over the group as a whole being the main focus. Correctional facilities and mental health services for those with personality disorders represent a spark in the movement of mental treatment, showing how pivotal any seemingly minor change can be in regards to a cure for those with ASPD. Any attempt to improve can be a future major turning point in disguise at the time. Due to the high cost of therapeutic communities, many have been closed down, leaving researchers to look into the direction of those taking place within hospitals and less obvious environments. There has been large progress within these types of atmospheres due to the fact that their focus has been shifted from contained punishment to behavior improvement and "post-inpatient" follow ups.

Although therapeutic communities demonstrated progress in the treatment of many mental disorders, they have shown a downfall in the progress of those with ASPD. Many treatment centers not only forgot about, but actively excluded those with ASPD from viable treatment options. This is due to the belief that they cannot undergo, or will end up refusing treatment. This goes to show how effective a motivating and optimistic treatment center can truly be, promoting a better potential mental state to each individual, and maximizing their own benefit as well as the benefit of the greater good within the community.

One example of an effective treatment center is the Arnold Lodge in the East Midlands. Arnold Lodge is a mental institution that keeps their patients in a secure environment while providing effective therapeutic care. Arnold Lodge does something that the criminal justice system does not. This institution focuses primarily on the personality disorders of previous offenders, effecting about ⅔ in totality, proving itself worthy of further inquisition.

Luckily, forensic psychiatric services have actually increased over the past two decades. This serves as a great example of progress in relation to these institutions. In many cases such as the Arnold Lodge mentioned above, they are proven effective due to the post-treatment measures reviewed. Offenders, it has been discovered, are less often re-admitted after attending these mental institutions and undergoing treatment. Although these centers may seem widely radical or progressive, their effectiveness can not be undermined. Institutions like these, oncs that primarily focus on personality disorders, provide a more specialized form of treatment over the majority of other centers that actively exclude these individuals. Services within these establishments include the improvement and focus on life skills, social problem solving and overall relapse prevention. They also consistently promote mindfulness, awareness of one's own actions as well as the consequences that follow them. At Arnold Lodge, specifically, patients have access to activities that may be therapeutic, such as animal care, woodwork, art creations and outdoor activities. This leads one back to the idea that the promotion of healthy activities proves itself extremely effective in improving each patient's life. Many of the foundations within these treatment centers follow the three stage model, including a high dependency treatment stage for complex patients at high risk. Low dependency treatment, on the other hand, involves the rehabilitation stage, focusing on long term improvement of behavior and post-institution lifestyles. Many of these various stages take place in a secure environment whose goal is to address the quality of life and maximize this quality, while minimizing one's risk or threat to the general public.

CHAPTER TEN – CURRENT ASPD TREATMENT OPTIONS

Although the public is ecstatic to coin terms like "psychopath" and "insane" they are not so quick to find treatments for those of the sort. Historically, treatments for those with ASPD have been questioned (and sometimes scorned) by the public. In reality, these programs are designed to maximize the usefulness of all individuals within society, as well as enforce the safety of the general public—not jeopardize it. Many of these programs, including attempted treatments within the criminal justice system, have been proven effective due to the fact that they have successfully reduced re-offending rates (Vanstone, 2000). These programs often focus on social work and the improvement of functions within a community in regards to how each individual shall behave. This has led to the increase of behavior and improving cognitive functions as the main goals of therapy.

As far as treatment centers in areas like the UK, most services are designed by the patients that had a motivation to change their behavior, thus shaping the very idea that these therapies revolve around. Many of these services, however, ended up excluding those with histories of substance abuse or violence. Not only is exclusiveness within treatment centers narrow-minded, but highly counterproductive as well, due to the fact that the deciding factors of ASPD include a constitution of these exact prevailing behaviors. Treatments shall be designed not to turn the other way and ignore severity, but to improve the already existing behavioral problems and decrease that severity. These issues shall be addressed, and it should be acknowledged that patients with severe cognitive or behavioral problems may be the *most* suited for these centers in the end. Furthermore, centers like these shall be viewed as places to provide compassion and hope for all affected individuals, no matter how hopeless they have been labeled. Take, for instance, Borderline Personality Disorder, which has seen great developments over the past decade from knowledge to patient treatment. BPD is the most common disorder treated within these centers, so it may be no coincidence that there have been drastic improvements made in the course of its treatment. This acts as a framework for how all personality disorders should be handled and improved among the course of designing treatment centers and utilizing different methods.

The myths surrounding ASPD are seldom challenged. With new possibilities of treatment emerging, that will all change. One admirable example is The Black Sheep Project, a center for patients with Borderline Personality Disorder in which its goal is not to merely attempt to provide treatment, but to act as a system in which the disorder can be effectively demystified. These foundations serve as stepping stones to eradicate the stigma as well as discover new aspects of the disorder and confirm new found knowledge.

These services are the beginning of a revolution. In regards to mental health, awareness will increase and resources will be provided for those affected, as well as their family friends. A positive outlook will be placed onto the fate of those affected.

The success of the treatment of ASPD is largely dependent on the changes within the criminal justice system. Some of the main factors that dictate the way that the judicial system handles criminal activity include the understanding and treatment of mental illnesses. Criminal activity, as a whole, is most of the time perpetrated due to an underlying personality disorder.

The criminal justice system, however, may serve as a loss of hope for the family and friends of those with ASPD and personality disorders as a whole. This is why the services that occur after one exits the criminal justice system are imperative to their future growth and success within society. One reason for the exclusion of those with ASPD includes the concern over their future danger towards the public. Services foster the belief that those with ASPD would be unresponsive towards any type of treatment. Yet, persons within these services continue to treat those with personality disorders as less treatable than the rest of the crowd. Even general facilities such as "local personality disorder services" left out those with ASPD, rightfully frustrating their family members and friends. Despite the overall exclusiveness within the realm of personality disorders, basic parameters were set in relation to how the treatment of ASPD should be conducted. Experts agreed that long term treatment is crucial, as well as staff possessing a flexible attitude towards each patient's individual needs. Patients must not only receive psychological help, but social help as well. By the end of treatment, staff must prepare patients to re-enter the world and every newfound aspect of their life as a whole after treatment is concluded. This is one of the many reasons as to why not only staff, but facilities and various services as a whole must form an overlying connection and work together.

Admission criteria to forensic security units include a diagnosis of a personality disorder that meets the criteria for detention under the mental health legislation. In regards to this diagnosis, the patient must present severe psychological or physical risk to society, requiring admission to security services for that reason. There must be a link between the personality disorder and the risk that one poses to the general public. This link must be clinically justified as well. Needs of the patient, in these cases, are said to be most effectively met in only the highest security environments.

Yet, it must be remembered that the vast majority of those with personality disorders function within an active community surrounding them. Although these individuals possess significant psychiatric malfunctioning and interpersonal difficulties, they are neglected from treatment. How will treatment be executed if one is only eligible *after* becoming an offender? Although post-treatment matters are worth pondering, the value of preventative measures must be taken into account as well.

Although a main function of forensic services is to provide treatment and reduce level of risk associated with antisocial behaviors, a survey conducted by The Eastern Specialized Mental Health Commissioning Group in 2005 found that admission criteria in these services often left out those with nothing but a diagnosis of ASPD. This exclusion is quite counterproductive, due to the fact that those with ASPD are seldom offered treatment until they become offenders in high security environments. For many of these forensic services, it has been suggested that admission criteria become more clear, as well as inclusive for all in need. Forensic services play a vital role in the fate of those with personality disorders. The teams within these environments provide advice to courts, links with the mental health services in prisons and often control the sentence or aftermath of one serving time.

The DSPD (Dangerous and Severe Personality Disorder) program assesses whether or not an individual has a personality disorder, as well as proceeds accordingly, meaning, providing treatment. The type and longevity of treatment is dependent on the individual and their own needs. Since the causes of ASPD may vary, as well as the degree of the disorder itself, treatment from person to person may have to vary as well. The need for more effort towards treatment, however, shall not remain static or up for debate, since the potential value can be clearly seen. That being said, common goals are shared within different systems. For instance, treatment strives to: reduce risk through behavioral therapy, figure out specific mental health needs through questioning, and create individualized treatment plans that maximize one's utility within society. Within these treatment plans, the staff that runs them is a crucial, deciding some of the main factors on how effective they will be. The Department of Health recommends that those who work with personality disordered patients must have extreme patience, interpersonal boundaries and a strong ability to tolerate the potential emotional impact of attempted treatment for the patients. Characteristics like these are important to note when the Department of Health delivers their people to DSPD units, as well as any unit of that matter attempting to deliver treatment. As mentioned earlier, a better understanding and deeper knowledge is beneficial for all, and shall be a vital, motivating factor that draws many closer to the goal of increasing education on personality disorders.

Not only is attempted treatment important within these services, but supervision alone is key to providing a nourishing environment for patients. Direct observation can have extensive benefits, some of which include: solidify whether or not the outcome of therapy matches the one desired, promote reliability and accountability of staff, keep close watch on patients and caretakers. Supervision has the power to increase the possibility of improvement at a more rapid speed than actions that would not otherwise be monitored or measured by any form. Monitoring these environments will ensure that patients are involved with a staff that cares about each individual and responds appropriately to each of their needs. This is especially pivotal in high-security environments, where the risk factors are high. Not only that, but there is a direct relationship between the security of the environment and the need to measure post-service improvement. Overall, these measures can create a productive stuff and prevent downfalls before they occur, as well as adjust any services as needed.

All in all, support from those running the services is of essence to those involved. Issues that often exclude those with ASPD from treatment services include the stigma of hopelessness and unwillingness to deal with the patients at all. Training and support as a whole will create clarity about personality disorders, as well as how to handle them, on the staff and patient's end.

The HM Inspectorate of Prisons in 2007 has recognized the truth that although the mental health needs of prisoners have been acknowledged, they have not been met. Although the main focuses include maximum security and post-release behavior, a shift in direction towards mental health problems would fix a large handful of other issues under the same umbrella that were mentioned before. Some have suggested dividing correctional facilities into specific wards, including some dedicated to those with a personality disorder. A prison constructed this way would, then, have wards dedicated to about ⅔ of its population. This, in itself, is evidence that ASPD is a substantial issue within the prison system, and in regards to almost all criminal activity. With that in mind, one can acknowledge that most prisons do in fact have Reasoning and Rehabilitation programs, which are focused on the improvement of behavioral as well as cognitive skills. Yet, it is important to note that these services focus on the offending behavior, and not the ASPD, which is the root of the behavior itself.

Effective treatment of those with personality disorders cannot be present in health care services without a close link to the criminal justice system. This is due to the fact that the individual begins "treatment", being treated by the professionals, the minute they become an offender. When leaving a high security system, it can be noted that post-jail time is a crucial moment in which one's behavior can be newly shaped in order to function more effectively. Since their primary care will come from jails or prisons, it is imperative that these systems are within close contact

with mental health facilities as well as the criminal
justice system in order to provide effective care for
each individual in regards to any stage that they are in
at the time. These systems must constantly be in
connection in order to provide a holistic treatment
plan for each patient overtime.

CHAPTER ELEVEN – INDIVIDUAL TREATMENT EXPERIENCES

In a survey conducted by Castillo in 2000, patients experiencing a personality disorder claimed that health services were seen as a last resort to them, and that the nature within the health services could be drastically improved. Some common problems mentioned included lack of respect or long term help. A surprisingly large number of patients suggested that "talking therapy" would be beneficial in the long run. Another common theme mentioned was a helpline, and that "out-of-hour services" would be useful and beneficial toward each patient's individual experience on top of any possible group work. That noted, it is logical to conclude that these individuals desire praise and rewards for their acceptable behavior as well as support from a large scale. An inclusive community has the potential to expedite the process of improvement. Overall, personality disorders are not often the focus within mental health services, thus contributing to the fact that these patients feel excluded from these organizations. Patients within the study that had previously been referred to specialist treatment spoke more positively and optimistically on the outcome of both therapy and medication.

That being said, in the 2002 study done by Haigh, many patients claimed that there was an over-reliance on drug treatment in regards to personality disorders. Not only that, but many individuals stressed the impact of early intervention beginning at a young age in order to prevent the manifestation of a personality disorder from the get-go. In regards to those with ASPD, social problem-solving therapies have proved to be extremely useful, since patients are often not aware of social cues or when to use certain social skills. It is likely that the education of social skills will engage the patients and lead them to more successful lives later on, informing them of how to act as a productive member of society. While many professionals believe that patients with personality disorders will be reluctant towards treatment, honing in on a social skill often sparks their interest. Aspects of therapy must promote their own growth and individual good, proving to them the possible long term benefits.

When patients experiencing ASPD (or other mental disorders, for that matter) are transferred from prisons to other, slightly lower security environments, their experiences seemed to share a common theme: resistance. Many of the offenders were hesitant to be transferred to other holding environments, yet were left with no choice. Although many patients dread the stages of treatment, the environment of hospitals has been widely reported as welcoming and nourishing towards their disorder. This has led many to believe that one of the most crucial factors within treatment environments was community. An overall sense of belonging and hospitality within an environment can motivate patients within the treatment centers to work towards a common goal, as well as see that their disorder does not only belong to them. Not only that, but these environments foster hope for the individual by allowing them to talk through their issues, versus solely being prescribed specific medications. While the staff and patient share the same goal, the patient is constantly receiving motivation and praise for any improvement to come, thus expediting the process of treatment.

One common problem within treatment is continued detention, and how long one should stay in treatment based on their improvement. Some feel that the more they talk about their disorder, the more reason for them to be kept in treatment. Due to this, many patients refrain from speaking with others about their mental disorders and put on a facade in order to appear as if they are responding well to the activities within treatment centers. Many feel that any sense of mental malfunctioning given off will be used against them and be seen as reason to keep them in the facility for a longer period of time. In fact, this issue became so detrimental from the patient's point of view that some have claimed that they would rather be in prison than a hospital, since with the hospital stay comes with it the notion that one's life will be filled with imprisonment in a mental institution from that point on. A lot of the time, patients befriend their doctors and fake their mental advancements for the sake of being released earlier than typical. Prisons and specialized hospital units need to implement more objective measures in order to be able to gage how long one's treatment should continue, as well as defining exactly which unit each patient belongs to, and for how long.

If the problems mentioned above continue on within the treatment centers, the consequences will be more disastrous than the current population can comprehend. If patients feel the need to fake their way through treatment, the treatment centers are manifesting even better and more clever, as well as manipulative, "psychopaths".

Other common complaints that exhibit the overall vibe given off within treatment centers include the notion that many nurses acted more as security guards than companions. One patient in Ashworth even described his detainment as "not therapeutic, but preventive", adding to the idea that these centers hold individuals not to improve their mental state for the greater good, but to prevent them from even having the opportunity to function properly in public settings, almost never mentioning the possibility of their release.

While prisons give punishments, treatment centers should be there to provide the opportunities for improvement. Treatment centers are facilities that allow patients to look at their crime, their own mental disorder, and foster ways to advance within society. While everyone in prison is viewed as a threat, patients within treatment facilities can be seen as similar counterparts… opportunities for growth… companions that one can discuss their mental disorder with. Prisons and their officers strive to keep the individuals away from the general public, while treatment centers should be places of growth that strive to exceed the mental state of each patient, allowing them to eventually re-enter the general public with a now higher functioning mindset. While access to treatment for personality disorders is increasing, the treatment centers themselves warrant closer investigation. More in-depth therapy groups are said to be highly effective by refusing to beat around any issues and confronting the direct problem of one's personality disorder at hand.

One popular treatment center is Grendon Underwood Therapeutic Prison, where they have implemented cognitive and behavioral techniques. This atmosphere consists of a therapeutic community of long-term offenders. Interestingly, these individuals are willing to inquire further about their behavior, as well as the behavior that has been inflicted upon them, and looking into that as a cause of their own habits. One anonymous individual in 2001 said "I have been given the time and space to work through and dismantle all the justifications and cognitive distortions I used to excuse not only the behaviour of those who abused me but also my own offending behaviour . . . I have learned to see others as people with feelings and rights of their own, and not just as bodies in which to take out frustration, anger or selfish gratification" (Castillo, 2003).

Programs like these must take into account the effect of personality on one's behavior, as well as implement many reformations in order to effectively humanize the individual once again. This enables patients to view themselves as flexible over stagnant. World views, as well as interpersonal perceptions, must be altered from beginning to end, thus proving that progress can be made. It will never be too late for one to seek out treatment once they see how their behavior can be altered, and life be improved.

A few prisoners have claimed that they had been able to control their aggression and violent behavior more effectively. One prisoner reflected that 'I've never, ever not been violent: trying or learning to control it is a major step for me. For 9 months I've not attacked anyone. You challenge yourself, but on these programmes, convicts challenge you also. But I've never previously taken criticism from anyone' (IMPALOX Group, 2007).

Fostering this type of hopeful and inclusive treatment environment also effectively expunges any potential fear of the patients before being admitted. Due to the stigma that follows the term "psychopath", many, ironically, fear for their own safety within centers of treatment. After all, these institutions are filled with, and only designed for those who have previously exhibited destructive behavior. However, many of these centers around the world, with the right professionals and environment, have been able to teach patients how to deal with their violent urges, eternal boredom and need to destruct. This type of atmosphere as a whole can help defeat the stigma as well, proving that the individuals within treatment can come out much better than before. With this idea constantly in the mind of the staff, patients will be motivated to be released by improving their own behavior as well as their own lives, rather than trying to merely gain the praise of their staff or achieve higher standards of living within these centers.

One way to get patients involved within their own treatment plans is to include them in the process of creating them. Not only will this motivate and engage the patient with activities of hopefulness, but it will accurately predict and assess the treatment that each individual will undergo, thus relieving their anxiety prior to beginning the plan. Identifying goals between the staff and patient can clarify what the patient should aim to do in order to improve their overall functioning, instead of keeping in the dark throughout the course of a one-sided treatment plan. Once the patient recognizes their specific behavioral or cognitive problems involving their personality disorder, each individual and staff can work collectively to design a unique treatment plan.

In order to progress one's self-sufficiency, those working with people with Antisocial Personality Disorder should allow the individual their own course of direction when assessing treatment plans. Staff not only can, but should be open to encouraging patients towards a variety of treatment options, specifically geared towards better understanding the reasons behind their actions as well as the potential consequences that follow up afterward. An optimistic, rewarding approach is more effective than a punishing one. Instilling the idea that treatment and improvement are possible gives the patient an incentive to want to go through with it in the first place, since those with ASPD are prone to withdrawing from treatment quite early, and in some cases, before it even begins. This is why it is necessary to immediately establish a purpose of treatment, as well as goals to work towards, and look forward to, for the future. Longevity of treatment should also be known by the patient, versus leaving them in the dark about how long they will be kept in the facility before release or transferal to another facility.

One must begin to ask themselves whether or not they truly believe that punishment can cure mental illness. If not, treatment deserves a second glance. Instead of questioning one's motive in regards to the crime they have committed, we must ask ourselves if the individual has lived a life of warning signs. It has been brought to public attention that often times, a white criminal's past is questioned, while those of other races are often seen as untreatable all together. It must be made clear: those of any race, gender, social class, etc. must be held equally accountable, and questioning one's harmful past shall not be a process of humanization, but a useful psychoanalytic tool in order to pinpoint the reckless beginnings.

While the rate of crime has significantly decreased over the past decade, fear of public violence and mass murders has gone up, and so have personality disorders. While crimes are often said to be caused by mental illness in grey terms, there is little talk about which mental illness is responsible for these crimes. There is also little to no recognition in regards to Antisocial Personality Disorder rising in the same fashion that public fear of widespread crime is. Offenders with ASPD do not need a motive, their drive to see the deterioration of their targets is enough on its own. It must be made clear what disorder is responsible, versus labeling any responsible individual as mentally ill and dismissing the case as it is. After all, this is the first step to viable and effective treatment. Not only is the general public ignorant as to which personalities are responsible for crime, but there is little awareness as to how charming they appear to be. Furthermore, the characteristics that constitute an individual with ASPD are subtle, almost invisible to the naked eye. Lack of judgment and social cues are the main factors, which then prove that the focus of professionals and the public should move away from their criminal history on its own. This is imperative to building a more preventative approach, as opposed to after the fact. Once the public is more educated on what makes one a sociopath/psychopath, the preventative approach will be on its way, and destruction will come to a halt before it is able to begin again.

Once public knowledge is developed, treatment will be as well. The idea that Antisocial Personality Disorder is merely involved within one's behavior and *not* their cognitive mental state must be eradicated. These individuals are experiencing an illness of the mind. Lower re-admitting rates after recovery can act as proof that positive treatment is out there, and will be a standpoint to build off of when counter-arguing a widespread stigma.

Lastly, it can once again be noted that the different areas and facilities of service should be in consistent contact with each other. Each system should communicate about the need to transfer an individual if necessary, as well as the identified goals and objectives as well as longevity of treatment. Networks being in contact with each other is critical to establishing each of their roles within the alternate stages of treatment. Down the road, this connection can also help when assessing the effectiveness of each operation within the units.

In an ideal situation, it would be common knowledge that one who has ASPD is not necessarily dangerous, but must be approached with caution and awareness. Once this manifests itself as a well-known fact, those with the disorder will no longer feel the need to put on a show. Most are not aware of how many problems this approach would take care of. Public awareness in regards to ASPD has the power to ease the misconceptions in regards to the mental illness. As for the professionals, extensive research can help determine ways to reduce the chances of those with ASPD to act on their drive, as well as see their target suffer, thus reducing crime.

It has been said about "psychopaths" in legal situations that these individuals commit more than twice as many violent crimes as other criminals. This is due to the fact that harm tends to be in their nature, and, in extreme cases, they are not able to predict the social repercussions that will occur as a consequence after the fact. Not only in regards to their consequences, but as for their target, they have no thought to the pain they inflict, since they have never experienced anything within the scope. They do not see violence or harm on a severe scale. They view them as nothing but actions used to ease their motivations, such as hunger or thirst—a simple drive. The aftermath of their behavior, although destructive to anyone involved, does not produce any effect on their being. They are more than likely to be indifferent and apathetic towards anyone they have inflicted pain upon. If not indifferent, they will be, at the least, satisfied at the result—the target that faces a long recovery ahead of them.

Being this "psychopath" is not a crime. Mental illness is not a crime. ASPD, in itself, is not a crime. Those who are brave enough to be open about their Antisocial Personality Disorder *before* it manifests itself into crimes shall face no harm or public shame, or fear any of the sort. The general public shall be aware that ASPD is nothing but a malfunctioning of emotions.

One shall not fear the psychopath, but instead be willing to work with them. This is the world that can be envisioned—a much safer one, to say the least. Most do not realize how much this would fix. One must not expect this to happen without effort, or rapidly, but it is possible for this shift to occur over a period of time. Through the efforts to educate society, the stigma can be wiped out. After all, this pattern has previously gone forth with other behaviors considered abnormal, that now seem to be widely accepted throughout all generations.

CHAPTER TWELVE – RAISING A STRONG CHILD

Although it is crucial to look at each individual's experience with ASPD, it would be naïve to view the disorder itself as a problem of individual perpetrators. Yet, many continue see these offenders as insane people who come out into the world, cause destruction and are quickly forgotten about afterwards. This does nothing but ignores the larger epidemic—ASPD is a widespread, and overly common illness. It demonstrates the effects of culture, raising children and behavioral ideals that are publicized. They are not always criminals, they are people that have been raised in a certain way. It is the very definition of manhood itself that may cause these problems.

"Be a man." "He is so strong, he's only cried a few times." These are just a few of the phrases that contribute to the disease in our society that happens to be most common in men. The stakes of this manifestation could not be higher. People spend time in prison due to this disease. Yet, no matter how much doubt, there *is* a solution to this epidemic. It involves a mixture of elements. Although the exact steps are hard to pin down, one can conclude that lots of trial and error will be needed. But one must be willing to recognize the components that make up harmful symptoms. Furthermore, one must be willing to feel vulnerable, as well as be held accountable. After all, these are what make up true power. One must not believe in the mantras, and continue to display emotions confidently—emotions that are not anger or hostility towards others. When one feels the need to feed their illness, they seek power. What they fail to recognize is that respect is power. It is nothing but early life experiences, or genetics, that allow one to objectify others so effortlessly. And while one's environment can influence their choices, it is their mind that dictates them. Certain institutions, primarily, group therapy, challenges the structures of these ways of thinking. These institutions can allow one to question not only the way that they act, but why they do so as well. Refusing to question's one's beliefs sends them on the path of the crowd, which is not powerful, in any sense. Mental health institutions can begin by urging one to question why they are thinking a certain way, only to end up at one answer: they have not been thinking in the first place. When asked who they are, these individuals will not have the ability to provide any answer to those seeking truth out of them.

Yet, the lack of response is truth in itself. Those who cannot provide answers for the way that they act end up weaker than others when undergoing states of potential vulnerability. Thus, they must recognize the places within their mind that are ready for transformation. Furthermore, it must be publicized that the real way to be tough is not to live up to this idea of manhood, but to challenge it—something only a real man could do.

When a baby is hungry, their mom gives them food. If a baby wants a diaper change, the parents change the baby's diaper. The caregiver of the child is the one catering to their needs. This process is part of the manifestation of who the child will turn out to be. How the caregiver responds to the child's needs has more of an impact than they will ever be able to comprehend. Every single, seemingly minor interaction that a parent has with their child is a building block in the formation of their future behavior. Through the development of attachment styles and levels of trust, it can be argued that raising a child is the most crucial point of growth in regards to their future. This is when the child discovers their sense of belonging, or not. This is also the time when they form attachments to their parents and get a sense of right and wrong. The early stages of one's life set the scene for how they will apply what they've learned in their adolescence and adulthood. Every face to face interaction that the child experiences is an indicator of how they will treat others later on. Those who are lucky enough to form a secure attachment to their caregivers tend to develop the needed/praised social and emotional skills later on in life. The unfortunate children, on the other side of the spectrum, may never be able to live up to that full potential… only some get that opportunity. Most of the time, these opportunities are uncontrollable, since they are manifested so early on in one's life and development. In order to build a strong attachment with one's child, the parents have to be determined. One must refuse to take the risk of raising a child with weak attachment styles. Parents must be empathetic, and listen to what their child has to say. It's important that they put themselves in their child's shoes frequently, as well as pay close attention, but it is not that obvious. Many parents do things that they don't realize can prevent their child, later on, from being able to reach their full potential. From being taught to repress one's emotions for years on end, an individual can actually develop the mechanisms that stop them from feeling those same emotions. The ways in which parents encourage their children to repress their emotional reactions are more common than spoken about.

Every time a parent tells their child, "quit crying", or "man up", they are relaying the message to the child that their own emotions are wrong. They are denying their pain, while the child continues to feel it. Even thanking the child for *not* crying about something teaches them to suppress their emotions. It is perfectly acceptable to praise one's child for not throwing a temper tantrum, but it is not acceptable to thank them for suppressing their emotions. Correcting their behavior, and teaching them what is socially acceptable and what is not should be a main goal of parenting. Their emotions, on the other hand, never need correcting. Once a child tells their parent how they are feeling, the parent then does not get to decide that the child is *not* feeling that way. The parent, instead, must deal with it by helping the child work through the emotion, not away from it all together. The only way out is through, so letting the child feel the emotion is the only safe way out. One must validate how their child is feeling, label it, and let them know that it is in fact okay. One must not force them to push their way around the feeling. Telling them to get over it or to not be nervous does nothing but minimize their pain. No matter how severe or mild a situation may seem on the parent's end, the child's emotion is valid. Parents must show empathy by letting their child know that they recognize how they feel. They must be able to teach their child that they can, in fact, act contrary to their emotions—like performing a poem on stage even if they are nervous. Providing praise for being brave and facing their fears (living through the emotion, and not suppressing it) will deem itself greatly effective later on towards their behavior.

While praising behavior is effective, it can be harmful as well. Praising the successful outcomes only is where most parents mess up. While it seems obvious to praise a child for their achievements, one must make it clear to their child that they will remain proud of them despite the outcome, and *because* of their effort. If, on the contrary, the parent convinces their child that they must succeed in order to gain the approval of the parents, they will end up hiding their mistakes instead of learning from them. Even worse, they will avoid any possibilities of failure in the future and later on in childhood. Avoiding any possibility of failure, although seems minor within childhood, can lead to a troubling personality in adolescence, leading to sociopathic tendencies such as extreme arrogance and emotional manipulation. The child may grow up to be extremely shallow if they are taught from a young age to repress any slightly uncomfortable emotional reactions. While it may seem like they are being raised to be emotionally strong, the child grows up to be a weaker individual in the end.

One must make it clear that the child's efforts are appreciated, and that despite the outcome of their behavior, the work they have put in has shown its value. Teaching them the value of their work allows them not only build a thick skin, but a useful work ethic as well. Letting the child fail and get rejected from time to time helps them take risks and step outside their comfort zones. Some parents instill the idea that failure must be prevented at all costs. But instead of correcting all of one's child's mistakes, it is important to communicate to them that failure is a part of life, and teaching them how to get back on their feet and cope with the failure afterwards is a skill that many miss out on. Building a mentally strong child is built off of this very foundation.

Many parents want to raise resilient children, but end up punishing their child more than *teaching* them. If a child is taught the skills and personality characteristics that will get them far in life, they will have those tools from a young age to guide them on hitting their full potential. When a child is constantly punished, nothing useful is done because nothing is ultimately learned. They will avoid failure, be afraid of authority, and remain ignorant on which qualities will lead them to success. Leaving them to figure these things out on their own is extremely detrimental for their future. Teaching them through words, and not just actions, is crucial.

The way that a parent interacts with their child can set the stage, and even stop a sociopathic trajectory in their child's life. As scary and uncertain this period may be, it requires more effort than ever. The activities that a parent does with their child—simply, how they spend their time—is an important stepping stone towards their ultimate fate. They must not be kept busy with mundane activities, or thrown on a couch to watch TV in solitude all day. Leaving a child alone with their devices sections them off from their peers, as well as prevents them from making new ones. Video games actually allow the child to see the world as a game, and treat people as objects. While this might sound far-fetched, a study done in 2013 by Robertson and colleagues found that the risk of being involved in the criminal justice system increased by about 30% with every hour that a child was on their TV.

Even common social activities, like school, are proven to be effective and impactful in the building of a child's social skills early on. One study done in 2013 by Monahan and colleagues shows that kids who went to school regularly and did not have a job showed the least antisocial behavior. On the other hand, the youths who did not attend school, yet worked for many hours on a regular basis were at the highest risk for Antisocial Personality Disorder. With that in mind, one can be led to conclude that school not only gives kids a social outlet, but acts a symbol of hope towards their future. They may find topics they are interested in and want to pursue through their education, as well as figure out who they want to be. School is a primary step towards helping a child become the person they want to be, and understanding their own personality on a more complex level.

The realization that one's child is a potential sociopath is a life-changing one. But the good news is, there are many preventative measures that can be taken early on with hope. Group therapy has the power to improve their social skills with other adolescents. Individual therapy has the potential to help the child feel their emotions while they still have them, versus suppressing them until they diminish. Although an understandable goal is for the child to care about others, it is equally important for them to care about themselves. This is why rewarding positive behavior is so important. Once a child recognizes that their behavior is appreciated, valued, and, at the least, socially acceptable, they are more likely to continue on with those actions. This is an extremely desirable outcome, since it is a huge indicator that their behavior is moving in the right direction. It then becomes highly unlikely for them to lash out in socially irresponsible ways. This also serves as proof that positive reinforcement manifests improvement more often than punishment or harsh words. One must act as if the problems are easily fixable, and that their child is completely capable of manifesting a change. One must show encouragement over doubt. Instead of making the child angry by lashing out onto them, rewarding them will increase the likelihood of their behavior serving towards the general good—collectively—such as, helping out another person. Rewarding functional behavior is a positive step towards the movement of their full potential, since it reinforces their ideas and models the way that their morals should be shaped. This also gives the child the image that they are a team with the parent, versus being controlled by the parent, thus, the child is not likely to feel angry towards the parent a lot of the time.

If a child is past the point of being able to behave in a social setting, there is still hope. Although the parents of these children may (rightfully) often feel the urge to give up on their child, the crucial stages of their life are not yet over. The essence of a child is not written in stone in their childhood, and any stage of their life seeks hope for improvement. It is difficult, yet not impossible, to be able to detach from one's child in states of uncertainty. It is extremely effective for the parent to let go of their own worries and emotions while dealing with their child, but it is necessary to objectively view their child as an opportunity for improvement. Although this is counterintuitive, it prevents the parent from acting out on their child or behaving purely on their instinctive emotions. While it would make sense to yell at one's child for behavior poorly in a public setting, parents can use that bad behavior as an opportunity to end the interaction in a state of connection with their child. This sends the message to the child that they are still loved, despite their problematic behaviors. If, on the other hand, the child feels that they won't be appreciated, no matter how they behave, they receive no motivation to be on good behavior, or terms with anyone else socially.

One reason that a rewarding environment is always more effective than a punishing one is since no treatment can breed a better human being by feeding into their "angry" nature. Instead of putting them in atmospheres that force them to survive as the perpetrators, an optimistic and rewarding environment can mold them into kind and compassionate humans, using their for praise can guide their behavior into eventually serving towards the greater good. Ensuring safety and promising improvement will motivate each individual to do so. Acting out in this certain way, that is, showing more empathy for others and acting out of kindness, also helps them to *see* the damage that can be done when one does *not* behave in this way. Many cognitive and behavioral therapies done in treatment can form empathizing individuals.

Although many of those with ASPD do not primarily engage in violence, *if* they are in a situation where someone could get hurt, they make sure to be the perpetrator. They see it as… any other option puts them in harm's way. They believe that putting in emotional energy is weak, so the emptiness must equal strength. But the greatest way to mask the fact that one lacks a sense of self is to put on a face of toughness, hiding behind a false sense of power. It will break. One's diseased value system will eventually come out to the forefront. When this happens, these old ways of thinking must be questioned. Ways of thinking, being, and reacting must be looked into deeply. Counseling and group therapy can prove powerful when comparing an individual before and after. Many, after the further inquisition of their structured beliefs, are able to experience emotions in a safe way. Being a real man involves characteristics that are defined as weaknesses. Emotional blindness is what allows others to be victimized. Although not all of the answers are comprehensive, new ways must be developed for men to show up into the world.

It is the definition of manhood that creates problems. It is believed that lack of emotion is a sign of strength. From a young age, it is instilled in children that *acting* tough—to put on nothing but a show—is how to be strong. Paradoxically, by doing this, parents are robbing their children of the opportunity to grow up and be mentally strong.

Children aren't born weak or tough. They are raised to be weak or tough. With parents' guidance and modeling of behavior, a child can grow up to be emotionally strong, which often doesn't look like how many envision it to. In fact, a study was done in 2003 within the 18-year-old men in the mandatory military service in Israel. It was concluded that the male adolescents who were raised in a non-nurturing environment coped *worse* through the "tough" military scene than those who were raised in a supportive, loving environment.

Toxic masculinity is created by culture. Boys are being taught to fit a stereotype—that if a boy fails to show masculinity in these certain ways, or behave in this fashion, they are not a "true man". The right way to be a man, as it turns out, does not exist. The gender of a person doesn't change their childhood experiences, socio-economic status, religion, or anything else regarding their mental thought processes. Some men like outdoor activities. Some like to read. Some get energy from hanging out with the guys, and some get energy from spending time alone. The problem is, the men who don't fit the stereotypical male are convinced by society that they are lacking.

Many men are taught to suppress a natural urge—anger. Later on in life, after years of being forced to hide their natural aggression, it comes out in *unnatural* ways. This is why, as children, it is vital to let boys, as well as girls, express their emotions through healthy behavior. This can help to redefine men's roles in society, and widen the scope of how they should behave. One must not hide or narrow the scope of toxic masculinity, but address it, and clarify what it really means to be a man. To be a man must be redefined. While people of different genders act differently, it might be less due to biological factors and more due to the societal norms that are so readily imposed on the children of today.

To begin education, the phrase toxic masculinity, as defined by The Good Men Project, is "a narrow and repressive description of manhood, designating manhood as defined by sex, status, violence and aggression. It is the cultural definition of manliness. Strength is everything while emotions are a weakness. Sex and brutality are yardsticks by which men are measured, while supposedly 'feminine' traits—which can range from emotional vulnerability to simply not being hypersexual—are the means by which your status as 'man' can be taken away" (The Good Men Project). This phrase was defined from research gathered in regards to studies done about men's violent behavior. It is important to note that it does not describe masculinity itself, but the gendered behavior. It describes the result of society defining what it means to be a man on such a narrow scope or set of behaviors.

While mental illness is responsible for the majority of crimes, one must dig deeper and ask what causes these disorders to not only start in the first place, but to increase from one generation to the next. Is there a gender component that warrants further attention? The majority of crimes are acted out by men. It would be shallow for one to assume that men are, naturally, more violent than women. It is a factor that differs between the way that girls and boys are raised. In a culture that equates masculinity with dominance and power over others, it isn't surprising that boys feel that they are failing at being a man if they don't act tough by being emotionless. Others must be given the space to express their gender in ways that feel authentic to

themselves, not in order to fit the societal norm of
what their gender is supposed to be.

Most are not born without compassion, they are
bred. Thus, they can be bred back. Compassionate
people can be made. Each patient *does* possess access
to the normal spectrum of human emotions that
children have, no matter how far out of if they may
seem. If one is desired to come out as a compassionate
being, they must receive that from the world as well.
One must not judge any child, or adult, for that
matter—for if one had their same upbringing and
genetic makeup, they would be the same way. After all,
early environments have the power to transform
individuals into someone they are not.

CHAPTER THIRTEEN – THE COSTS OF ASPD

Not only is the financial burden large in regards to the individual with ASPD, but the cost of treating their victims is substantial as well. The criminal justice system houses these individuals within the correctional facilities, as well as provides security and law enforcement as a whole. Attempting to provide treatment, whether that be therapy or medicine, poses a separate cost. Although no exact number is known in regards to how much ASPD costs, it is correct to conclude that it is to a great degree.

Setting monetary values aside, the social consequences of Antisocial Personality Disorder affect society at large. These individuals are responsible for a wide range of offenses, including violent behavior and crime as a whole. They are extremely heavy within prison populations. One study of prisoners across the world found that 47% of men and 21% of women (in prison) had Antisocial Personality Disorder. This goes to show that although many will continue to question the criminal's motive, they should question their lifelong behavior instead. Studies on prison populations in different nations have found varying numbers in regards to how many have personality disorders, yet they are always substantially high. Despite the fact that ASPD is responsible for most offenses, there is little public recognition.

If one with ASPD does not end up in a correctional facility, they still pose harm to family and friends. While they may not be violent, their manipulation tactics will get the best of their targets, as previously discussed. Even if these individuals do not actively harm their colleagues, their caregivers will experience a great deal of stress and little progress. In fact, caregivers of those with Antisocial Personality Disorder have reported higher levels of depression and hopelessness than the caregivers for those of different mental illnesses. The severity often goes unnoticed.

With that being said, one who has ASPD themselves is also at risk when it comes to health issues and life outcome as a whole. Studies have shown that those with ASPD are at increased risk for schizotypical, borderline, and other personality disorders later on in their lives. Although many of these conditions can be treated through therapy or medication, the ASPD alone prevents them from ever seeking or acknowledging the fact that they need help. People with ASPD are less likely than those with other disorders to seek treatment, since they see nothing wrong, and demonstrate their indifference with apathy. They are offset, neutral, and will not act to increase even their own well-being, since, often times, they see nothing wrong with their current state. These individuals are more likely to use drugs and alcohol. One study proved that even though 12% of the general population smoke, more than half of those with ASPD are smokers. This increased risk of developing other disorders later on in life may be due to their risk-taking behavior and disregard for their own personal safety. Also, evidence has shown that mental health problems are risk factors for physical diseases as well. In a long-term US study, those with ASPD had a higher risk of diseases like liver disease, coronary artery disease, and arthritis. On top of that, these individuals were six times more likely than the average person to be hospitalized and twice as likely to visit the ER. Although the cause of these risks are not entirely known, their behavior plays a pivotal role, and increases their chances of downfall significantly.

Life outcomes, in general, for those with Antisocial Personality Disorder fall far from the norm. Although it is known that they are unlikely to hold down a long term relationship or job, it goes unnoticed that they are also more likely to rely on government disability income and food assistance programs. They are also less likely to ever attain a college degree, and attend college as a whole. These individuals, most often, do not have friends. If they do, it is not a deep relationship, but a mere acquaintanceship in disguise as friendship to supplement their overall image. Even with their immediate family, they do not seek help in

regards to their disorder, since they see no reason to—
they do not see Antisocial Personality Disorder as a
disorder, but a social advantage. Looking towards the
end, people with ASPD have a higher risk of
premature death. One study of 500 participants found
that these individuals were 8 times more likely to die
than individuals with different conditions. Causes of
this risk include reckless behavior and indifference
towards dangerous situations. Another important
factor is fight or flight—which is, as can be recalled,
non-existent in these individuals.

CONCLUSIONS

We, as a collective society, should not only strive to consider the behaviors that constitute ASPD, but the internal mental processes, as well as the factors that first bring the disorder to life. One is capable of functioning as a giving, productive individual *if* not born with Antisocial Personality Disorder. It is easy to see the potential in many of them. It is not hard to understand that the individual with ASPD lives a life so far from normal, since their mind functions so far out from typical. Not only that, but their behaviors constitute a lifestyle that most do not follow. Their pattern is easy to follow. Often times, they end up in correctional facilities, denied of treatment, and never knowing what it is like to feel remorse or empathy. The truth being, that they do not know what they are missing, and due to lack of treatment, never will. They view the world as a game, and people as objects. With that in mind, one can decide whether or not the individual is deserving of empathy. If, as studies suggest, these individuals are *born* with a predisposition towards abnormal behavior, one can conclude that it is not their fault. If, biology is a factor in the creation of ASPD, one can understand that their upbringing is responsible. And last, if their environment instills those abnormal behaviors within them, we can conclude that they do not, after all, have complete control over their behavior. If, in the future, knowing someone with ASPD is the norm, we can picture them as a child instead of seeing them as they are now… a child who has been exposed to a habitat that has shaped them into the way they are now. Through further investigation, we can find the balance between pitying someone, and realizing that they need our help. They are not evil, they are mentally ill. The larger issue is that they are human, but not fully.

Some may find it unfathomable that those with ASPD view themselves as superior because of their disorder, but that is the truth. They argue that life is easiest with Antisocial Personality Disorder, and without all of the emotions. But the shallow people, to state it plainly, just don't get it. They live their entire lives without understanding the entities that surround them. They think of themselves as morally superior because they don't have an opinion on anything, which, paradoxically, makes them cowardly. It's said that the light is on, but nobody is home. And the reason that one lacks depth is because they don't seek it. These individuals are perfectly content with their surface level lives, and don't have the urge to investigate further, or live a well-nourished, experienced life. Rather, they attempt to occupy their empty mind with crafty manipulation tactics that promote the destruction of the other party. At the end of the day, that is a very unfortunate place to be.

The superficial, shallow affect that these individuals possess shall never be underestimated. The person who fails to recognize others' emotions are the ones who do not have their own. Poor behavioral conduct. Inability to feel genuine love. Shallow emotions. These are just a few of the characteristics that toxic masculinity, the patriarchy, pop culture, and social media readily respond to. They also make up Antisocial Personality Disorder. In fact, the characteristics above were extracted from the DSM.

It is vital to comprehend the truth. Those who are shallow take life as it is. They do not want to make it anything else—anything more developed. Without trouble, they seem to freely go through the motions, making the most out of their circadian routine. At last, they will become worn out from tirelessly chasing meaningless aspects of life—attempting to derive happiness from things that have no purpose. It is only at that moment that they begin to ponder. Never once have they pondered, but now they do. The only difference is: time is up. There is nothing left for them, since they have wasted it all. They are constantly on the move, trying to reach anything that gives them any amount of pleasure. It is as a result of this that they experience pleasure more often than the deep person. Fullness—duration—however, cannot be promised, since they jump from one entity to the next, without a thought, attempting to seek any level of pleasure. Their opposite counterparts are constantly pondering over what has occurred—unable to move from one thing to the next so rapidly. These types of people often do not seem as content, and as their pondering continues, they begin to see the world as it is. While in the moment it seems trivial, the epiphany is manifested when one begins to realize that joy cannot be derived from external factors. Because of this, these people learn to construct their own happiness from within— through their mindset. This is a form of intelligence so underrated… so unfathomably valuable. If, at the end of countless years, one takes a step back to highlight the contrasts between the deep and shallow, they find that the deep person is the content one. The deep person is the one that is able to cherish each emotion—they are able to ponder them, and the ability to ponder is a gift, for one can derive happiness from things that cease to exist. While the shallow person experiences such an absurd level of obliviousness, not only are they incapable of manifesting joy from nothing, but they cease to notice what is right in front of their eyes.

Allow me to proceed… I am going to leave you with one last thought. Do not interact by asking people what they believe to be true… they will fail to articulate their true inner workings. Words cannot do that for them. Words are never sincere. Feelings are. Even as one believes he is expressing his deepest sorrows, what ends up coming out is polished and over-rehearsed. But enclosed within the spoken language, the feelings are kept. Through listening, they can be found. So listen to one another. You cannot force one to open up about how they truly feel, in case they are not willing to do so at that moment. But you can be a listener… a seeker. Even then, one may prefer small talk. They keep it uncomplicated—surface level. Allow them. That is a reflection upon themselves. Allow their simplicity. Embrace it. It will soon be discovered that their feelings will pour out, in one form or another, and not always in the ways that we expect.

Ultimately, much about Antisocial Personality Disorder remains inconclusive. We are learning a great deal. Thankfully, loads of research is being conducted, and what we once thought we knew is evolving into deeper, more empathetic understandings. Indeed, we will continue to learn more about personality disorders as the research goes on. Even studies done in recent years are uncovering hidden knowledge. Many papers have boldly included "overcoming ASPD" within their very titles. Perhaps, the man with Antisocial Personality Disorder has a mind that can overcome all he has been accustomed to. As we navigate the vast world of research, it will be nourishing to encounter the new findings along the way.

WORKS CITED

Andersen, Allan M., et al. "1.26 Elopement Patterns And Caregiver Strategies." *Journal of the American Academy of Child & Adolescent Psychiatry*, vol. 55, no. 10, 2016, doi:10.1016/j.jaac.2016.09.027.

Aram, Liz. "Mental Health Is a Mainstream Issue for Employers, Says Campaign." *PsycEXTRA Dataset*, 2001, doi:10.1037/e427012008-006.

"Arnold Lodge Nottinghamshire Healthcare ." *NHS Choices*, NHS, www.nottinghamshirehealthcare.nhs.uk/arnold-lodge.

"Black Sheep Project." *Black Sheep Project*, www.blacksheepproject.org/.

Black, Donald W. "The Natural History of Antisocial Personality Disorder." *Canadian Journal of Psychiatry. Revue Canadienne De Psychiatrie*, The Canadian Psychiatric Association, July 2015, www.ncbi.nlm.nih.gov/pmc/articles/PMC4500180/.

Brook, Michael, et al. "Psychopathic Personality Traits in Middle-Aged Male Twins: a Behavior

Genetic Investigation." *Journal of Personality Disorders*, U.S. National Library of Medicine, Aug. 2010, www.ncbi.nlm.nih.gov/pmc/articles/PMC4438762/.

"Case Studies." *Antisocial Personality Disorder - Home*, serial-killing.weebly.com/case-studies.html.

Diagnostic and Statistical Manual of Mental Disorders. American Psychiatric Publishing, 2013.

DSM-II: Diagnostic and Statistical Manual of Mental Disorders. The Association, 1968.

Dunbar , Edward. *Program Considerations for Clients with Antisocial Personality Disorder*, 2016, Counseling.org.

Eng, J, and U R Nair. "Left Ventricular Outflow Tract Obstruction from Mitral Prosthesis." *International Journal of Cardiology*, U.S. National Library of Medicine, Mar. 1991, www.ncbi.nlm.nih.gov/pubmed/2055678.

Friedman, Howard S. *Encyclopedia of Mental Health*. Academic Press, 2016.

Gawda, Barbara. "The Emotional Lexicon of
Individuals Diagnosed with Antisocial Personality
Disorder." *Journal of Psycholinguistic Research*,
Springer US, 2013,
www.ncbi.nlm.nih.gov/pmc/articles/PMC3825036/.

"Grendon Prison Information." *Justice.gov.uk*, 19
Feb. 2019, www.justice.gov.uk/contacts/prison-
finder/grendon.

"Important Differences Uncovered between US and
Dutch Psychopaths." *Research Digest*, 7 Feb. 2018,
digest.bps.org.uk/2018/02/07/important-differences-
uncovered-between-us-and-dutch-psychopaths/.

"Index to International Journal of Offender Therapy
and Comparative Criminology Volume
49." *International Journal of Offender Therapy and
Comparative Criminology*, vol. 49, no. 6, 2005, pp.
728–733., doi:10.1177/0306624x0504900610.

Lessig, Lawrence. "Social Meaning and Social
Norms." *University of Pennsylvania Law Review*,
vol. 144, no. 5, 1996, p. 2181.,
doi:10.2307/3312651.

"Life with Antisocial Personality Disorder (ASPD)." *Life with Antisocial Personality Disorder (ASPD) | Mind, the Mental Health Charity - Help for Mental Health Problems*, www.mind.org.uk/information-support/your-stories/life-with-antisocial-personality-disorder-aspd/#.XIeMNy3Myu4.

National Collaborating Centre for Mental Health (UK). "ANTISOCIAL PERSONALITY DISORDER." *Antisocial Personality Disorder: Treatment, Management and Prevention.*, U.S. National Library of Medicine, 1 Jan. 1970, www.ncbi.nlm.nih.gov/books/NBK55333/.

Riley, Michael, and JH Bloomberg School of Public Health. "Origins of Mental Health." *Johns Hopkins Bloomberg School of Public Health*, 7 Nov. 2013, www.jhsph.edu/departments/mental-health/about-us/origins-of-mental-health.html.

Robertson, Lindsay A, et al. "Childhood and Adolescent Television Viewing and Antisocial Behavior in Early Adulthood." *Pediatrics*, American Academy of Pediatrics, Mar. 2013, www.ncbi.nlm.nih.gov/pmc/articles/PMC3581845/.

Yell, Nicole. "The California Sexually Violent
Predator Act and the Failure to Mentally Evaluate
Sexually Violent Child Molesters." *GGU Law
Digital Commons*,
digitalcommons.law.ggu.edu/ggulrev/vol33/iss2/7/.

Zhong, Baoliang, et al. "Prevalence of Antisocial
Personality Disorder among Chinese Individuals
Receiving Treatment for Heroin Dependence: a
Meta-Analysis." *Shanghai Archives of Psychiatry*,
Shanghai Municipal Bureau of Publishing, Oct.
2014,
www.ncbi.nlm.nih.gov/pmc/articles/PMC4248258/.

www.ingramcontent.com/pod-product-compliance
Lightning Source LLC
Chambersburg PA
CBHW071225240726
48654CB00009B/925